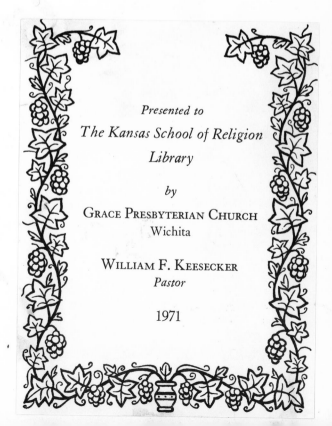

Mark—
Traditions in Conflict

MARK—
TRADITIONS in
CONFLICT

THEODORE J. WEEDEN

FORTRESS PRESS   PHILADELPHIA

Library of Congress Catalog Card Number 70-157543

ISBN 0-8006-0041-X

1934C71   Printed in U. S. A.   1-41

Bible, N.T. Mark - Criticism, interpretation, etc

To Jane

and

Scott, Ted, Michael, Brian, Anne

Contents

ABBREVIATIONS

AJT	*American Journal of Theology*
EvTH	*Evangelische Theologie*
HTR	*Harvard Theological Review*
Int	*Interpretation*
JBL	*Journal of Biblical Literature*
JBR	*Journal of Bible and Religion*
JR	*Journal of Religion*
JTC	*Journal for Theology and the Church*
JTS	*Journal of Theological Studies*
Nov Test	*Novum Testamentum*
NTS	*New Testament Studies*
RGG	*Die Religion in Geschichte und Gegenwart*
ST	*Studia Theologica*
TDNT	*Theological Dictionary of the New Testament*
USQR	*Union Seminary Quarterly Review*
ZNW	*Zeitschrift für die neutestamentliche Wissenschaft*
ZTK	*Zeitschrift für Theologie und Kirche*

Preface

The thesis presented in this book first occurred to me toward the end of my doctoral studies at Claremont Graduate School and University Center and became the subject of my doctoral dissertation, "The Heresy That Necessitated Mark's Gospel," in 1964. Since that time the thoughts first expressed in the dissertation and later summarized in my article "The Heresy That Necessitated Mark's Gospel" (ZNW 59 [1968]: 145–58) have been refined and expanded and have finally evolved into this book. In a project such as this, when one strikes out on new, uncharted paths in Markan interpretation, he does so with a sense of exhilaration and sobriety—exhilaration caused by the excitement over the discovery of new insights and sobriety caused by the recognition that further critical reflection will undoubtedly point up the need for modification and refinement of the conclusions drawn from these insights. The reader will soon note that there are gaps in this treatment of Mark, that there is much that needs to be explored which was not explored in this work. To an extent publication limitations make this necessary; to a larger extent some fruitful areas of analysis were passed up because they lay outside the scope and intention of this project. With this in mind, the interpretation of the Markan *Sitz im Leben* herewith proffered is not presented as a final statement on Mark. What I present is a working hypothesis that I believe will contribute to a better understanding of the purpose behind the writing of the first Gospel and which I believe will serve as a useful point of departure for continued investigation of the Markan problem.

My indebtedness to others is legion. It is not possible to cite all who have given helpful suggestions and critical response to my thinking. Special words of appreciation must be penned to the following. I am particularly indebted to two of my teachers, James M. Robinson and Ernest C. Colwell. James Robinson was the first to open my eyes to the excitement of the serious, critical study of the New Testament when I was a student at the Candler School of Theology, Emory University. Later he guided my critical encounter with the New Testament during my graduate studies at Claremont Graduate School. His perceptive and provocative insights served as the catalyst for the thesis of this book.

Ernest C. Colwell gave generously of his time and attention to my study while I was his student both at Emory University and Claremont Graduate School. His counsel during the course of my doctoral program at Claremont was invaluable. It would be difficult to find one who embodies to a greater degree the warmth and genuineness of the Christian spirit.

I am indebted to Crozer Theological Seminary (now merged with Colgate Rochester Divinity School/Bexley Hall), and particularly its dean, R. Melvin Henderson, for providing secretarial assistance and support in the preparation of the manuscript. My thanks are also due to my colleague Jesse H. Brown, student assistant Ronald Wright, and student Alan Clark for reading the manuscript and making helpful suggestions.

Finally, words do not fully express the indebtedness I owe to my wife, Jane, and my children who have sacrificed much in support of my completion of this work.

Introduction

The Problem of Markan Interpretation: How and Where to Begin

The advent of redaction criticism has come as a breath of fresh air to Markan scholarship stagnated by the restrictions of previous methodological presuppositions and procedures.[1] Redaction criticism has placed in our hand the key for unlocking the mysteries behind the Gospel of Mark and its creation. All that need be done is to separate Markan redaction from the evangelist's working material, extrapolate the Markan mind from the redactional parts of the Gospel, and we can then answer all the questions related to the composition and purpose of Mark.

One would wish the task could be so simply accomplished! For while the redaction-critical premise that Mark exercised an author's freedom and creativity in composing the Gospel is a sound postulate with which to begin a Markan study, such a position has the effect not only of providing the key to the Markan mysteries but also of opening a Pandora's box of exegetical and hermeneutical problems. In past attempts to explain the Gospel these problems have been kept more manageable because it was assumed that the evangelist's literary and theological in-

1. For a survey of Markan scholarship prior to the emergence of redaction criticism, cf. Vincent Taylor, *The Gospel According to Mark* (London: Macmillan and Co., 1959), pp. 1–25, 67–77, and James M. Robinson, *The Problem of History in Mark* (Naperville, Ill.: Allenson, 1957), pp. 7–20. For a discussion of redaction criticism and redaction-critical investigations of Mark, cf. Joachim Rohde, *Rediscovering the Teaching of the Evangelists*, trans. D. Barton (Philadelphia: Westminster Press, 1968) and Norman Perrin, *What Is Redaction Criticism?* (Philadelphia: Fortress Press, 1969).

volvement in his composition was limited. If one operated on such an assumption it became relatively easy to arrive at a plausible explanation of the Gospel. One just combined the results of the form-critical investigation of the oral tradition with the insights of Wilhelm Wrede and Martin Kähler to explain Mark. The evangelist was then seen to have brought together various individual units of preliterary (or literary) material of identifiable genres (form criticism), linked them together with a theological theme, the messianic secret (Wrede),[2] and affixed the resulting conglomeration as an introduction to an already fully developed passion narrative (Kähler).[3]

Redaction criticism opens Pandora's box when it concedes so much freedom to Mark as an author. No longer can the pieces of the Markan puzzle be so easily delineated and differentiated; no longer can an explanation of the Gospel be so simply pieced together. In postulating a much freer hand for Mark in the composing process, redaction makes the lines which are drawn by form criticism between Markan created material and Markan received material look less sharply defined, the distinctions less assured. That is not to say that the preliterary genres identified in Mark by the form critics suddenly evaporate. They are still there, clearly recognizable. They offer indisputable evidence that a large amount of the material in the Gospel existed independent of Mark as isolated units, units which were used by Mark as the building blocks for his own literary construction. What is brought into question is the extent to which these various genres may have been reworked by Mark for his own purpose. To put it another way, as long as one limits the role of the evangelist to that of an editor, one can assume that he has for the most part reproduced his material untouched, exhibiting

2. See William Wrede, *Das Messiasgeheimnis in den Evangelien*, 3d ed. (Göttingen: Vandenhoeck and Ruprecht, 1963).
3. See Martin Kähler, *The So-called Historical Jesus and the Historic, Biblical Christ*, ed. and trans. C. E. Braaten (Philadelphia: Fortress Press, 1964), p. 80.

his own particular biases only at those points where his editorial hand was required to link the received material together in some meaningful composite. Operating under such an assumption it is a fairly simple matter to separate tradition from redaction and identify Markan fingerprints.

But if one is to permit the evangelist the freedom and creativity of an author, then one cannot deny him the option of exercising that freedom in the reworking of the content of his received material, as well as in the piecing together of the material. Certainly Matthew and Luke exercised such freedom in their use of Mark. Once one is aware of such a possibility, it is not always easy to make judgments as to what is tradition and what is redaction. It is not so easy to draw boundary lines around the contextual limits of Mark's redactional activity.

Likewise, when one posits in the evangelist's hands such literary creativity and control over his material, one must ask if his theological ingenuity can be limited simply to his incorporation of a kerygmatic motif (the messianic secret) as a theme embracing all his material. Is it not possible that his theological interests are more sophisticated than merely the tying together of his material with a borrowed theme? Recent examination of the secrecy motif in Mark indicates that it plays a much more complex role in the Gospel than previously perceived.[4] This fact along with the recent exposure of Mark's skillful assimilation of two contrasting christologies in his work[5] suggests that Mark is a much more deliberate theologian than had earlier been assumed. To limit his theological interest to

4. See, for example, Ulrich Luz, "Das Geheimnismotiv und die Markanische Christologie," ZNW 56 (1965): 9–30.

5. See Johannes Schreiber, "Die Christologie des Markusevangeliums," ZTK 58 (1961): 154–83 and idem, Theologie des Vertrauens (Hamburg: Furche-Verlag H. Rennebach K. G., 1967); James M. Robinson, "The Recent Debate on the 'New Quest,'" JBR 30 (1962): 203–4; Leander Keck, "Mark 3:7–12 and Mark's Christology," JBL 84 (1965): 341–58; Eduard Schweizer, "Zur Frage des Messiasgeheimnisses bei Markus," ZNW 56 (1965): 1–8; Luz, "Das Geheimnismotiv," pp. 9–30; and Helmut Koester, "One Jesus and Four Primitive Gospels," HTR 61 (1968): 230 ff.

the superimposing of the messianic secret to provide
literary and theological cohesiveness for his narrative is to
look at the Gospel with monocular vision.

Yet postulating such theological creativity on the part
of the evangelist complicates further an already difficult
hermeneutical problem. If as a theologian Mark exercised
the freedom to shape his composition according to his purpose, how can one clearly distinguish between the inherent
theological interests of the various units of his material and
Mark's own interests in incorporating this material into his
composition and in creating the Gospel?

If the separation of tradition and redaction is not as
easily achieved as previously thought because of the in-
creased freedom assigned to the author, how can a methodology be devised that will enable us to isolate accurately
specific concerns of the evangelist and help us, through the
aid of those concerns, to interpret the Gospel correctly?
In the case of Matthew and Luke the task is not as difficult as it is for Mark. At least one possesses one of their
sources (Mark) prior to its assimilation into their Gospels.
One can gain some fairly assured insights into their particular interests by examining the way in which they use
that source. Markan scholars are not blessed with such a
luxury. They do not possess the evangelist's received material independent of its existence in the Gospel.

Mark could have saved us a lot of frustrating and fruit-
less hermeneutical work following leads down blind alleys
if somewhere he had just stated straightforwardly the
origin of his Gospel and described the situation in his
church that inspired its creation; or, barring that, if he had
just given us some clear clues as to how we should interpret
his work. But no such assistance comes from our evangelist.
He remains eternally silent, leaving us to devise our own
means for uncovering his purpose and the situation in his
community that required him to take up his pen and write.

Without help from the evangelist and without clear-cut
knowledge of his sources, devising a methodology that will
take us to the heart of the Markan purpose is an extremely

difficult task. Efforts to develop such a methodology have been a matter of first priority ever since 1956, when Willi Marxsen broke ground in this area in his book *Der Evangelist Markus.*[6] To Johannes Schreiber must go the credit for making one of the most significant contributions in this direction. Schreiber worked out the following procedural principles for unraveling the Markan problem.[7]

(1) All verses of Mark that are to be ascribed to Mark's redaction on the basis of the methods of analytical research provide the point of departure for establishing his theology, to the extent that a unified theological conception becomes visible in spite of the fact that these verses are scattered over the whole Gospel.

(2) Where Matthew or Luke or indeed both alter the text of Mark at a given point, especially if this is carried through the whole Gospel, we very probably have to do with a theological Markan statement which they reject. This principle is especially valid where it can be shown that their own theology contradicts that of Mark on this point.

(3) The selection and arrangement of the tradition in Mark also permits inferences as to the evangelist's redaction.

(4) Markan theology as established on the basis of these principles must not only produce a message consistent in itself, but it must also be meaningful in terms of a given situation in the history of religion.[8]

Schreiber has performed an important service for Markan scholarship in outlining these principles. No study of Mark

6. Eng. tr. *Mark the Evangelist,* trans. R. A. Harrisville et al. (Nashville, Tenn.: Abingdon Press, 1969).

7. Schreiber, "Die Christologie," pp. 154–55. See also his discussion in *Theologie,* pp. 1–21. The initial attempt by Marxsen (*Mark,* pp. 15–29) to work out an appropriate redaction-critical methodology for Markan study did not spell out such principles as carefully as Schreiber has done, although Schreiber's principles lie implicitly, if not explicitly, behind Marxsen's study.

8. English translation of these principles is by James M. Robinson, "The Problem of History in Mark, Reconsidered," *USQR* 20 (1965): 134.

is now on sound footing if it is not guided by such principles. But in and by themselves they offer an inadequate
methodology for the resolution of the Markan problem.
Because of the inherent weaknesses they possess and because of their failure to go far enough at certain crucial
points, they still do not provide us with sufficient directions out of the hermeneutical maze in which Markan
scholarship finds itself.

Let me illustrate what I mean. First of all, Schreiber's
second principle, which argues that joint Matthean and
Lucan alteration of Mark signals Matthean and Lucan
reaction to specific Markan prejudices, has its Achilles'
heel. Undoubtedly, there are instances in which both
Matthew and Luke alter the Markan text in objection to
Markan theology. But, as James Robinson[9] has pointed
out, on some occasions where this takes place the alteration may not identify their correction of Markan theological prejudices. It may be accounted for by their own
theological intention to move away from the "authentic"
tradition as Mark presents it to a position more in keeping
with the interest of the church in their time. Corrections
may reflect post-Markan doctrinal changes in the understanding of the disciples, the church, and christology. Or
in some cases they may reflect Matthew's and Luke's consciousness that Mark's poor Greek needs revision.

This flaw in Schreiber's hermeneutical guideline in no
way discredits its usefulness. It can be quite valuable in
helping to isolate the peculiarities of Mark. But it must
be applied with caution. Final judgment as to whether
Markan traits (isolated by the comparison of Matthew
and Luke with Mark) point to a peculiarly Markan bias
must rest on the support of other data gathered through
analytic study. In this regard three coordinates are extremely important for helping to arrive at such judgment:
(1) a knowledge of the peculiar theological twists of
Matthew and Luke, (2) a knowledge of the theological
concerns of the church before and after Mark, and (3)

9. Robinson, "The Problem . . . Reconsidered," p. 135.

insights about Mark offered by other Markan redactional characteristics, isolated by means other than a comparison of Mark with its synoptic successors.

The weakness in Schreiber's third principle is the question of the evangelist's principle of selectivity. The conclusion that he ignored or chose not to include more material (e.g., the teaching of Jesus) presupposes that he had such material in his possession, making it possible for him to exercise the option of ignoring what did not suit his purpose. Such a presupposition has yet to be proved.[10]

The most important of Schreiber's methodological principles is the first. Its functional goal cannot be faulted. But its shortcoming is that it really leaves us in the lurch. It fails to tell us how we are to evaluate the relative merits of the data that are gathered as a result of its implementation, and how to arrange these data for interpretation so that we can have some measure of confidence that a reconstruction of the origin and purpose derived from them is on target with the evangelist's intent. Schreiber tells us we are to look for a visible, unified theological conception to emerge from isolating peculiarly Markan characteristics in the course of our investigation of the Gospel. But does such a visible, unified theologian's conception naturally arise as a result of the pieces of data falling into place of their own accord? Or are not the unity and visibility of such a theological conception really imputed to the material by the mind of the investigator, who sees in the amassing of data what he wants to see?

To illustrate the problem, as a result of the application of Schreiber's first principle present Markan scholarship tends to identify the following as significant characteristics of Mark: (1) the messianic secret, (2) the persistent obtuseness of the disciples, (3) the evangelist's use of material from a *theios-aner* (divine-man) tradition, (4) the structural arrangement of the Gospel in units organized around motifs such as the call to discipleship, summary statements on Jesus' ministry, conflict, passion, and so on,

10. Robinson, "The Problem . . . Reconsidered," p. 135.

and (5) the emphasis on suffering christology and disciple-ship.[11] A large number of scholars, influenced by Wrede, assume that the hermeneutical theory which provides com-posite meaning for all these Markan peculiarities is the messianic secret. But what dictates that the starting point for the understanding of Mark must be the messianic secret?[12] Why should it not be the Markan presentation of the disciples, the possible partitioning of the Gospel into sections, or some other Markan peculiarity identified by careful critical analysis? The hermeneutical point of departure one chooses is of critical importance. For the redactional element or hermeneutical principle selected as the starting point for interpreting the Gospel obviously affects how one approaches the Gospel and determines in large measure one's explanation for it. A few examples will establish the point.

Willi Marxsen takes his cue for an approach to Mark from Kähler's thesis that the Gospels are passion narratives with long introductions. He theorizes that the Jesus tradi-tion must have developed backwards. Complexes of ma-terial are prefixed to other complexes of material. The former, strangely enough, serves as commentary on the latter. Thus Marxsen argues that the place to begin the study of Mark is the first pericope. It acts as the initial commentary on what follows and serves as the paradig-

11. On the obtuseness of the disciples, see particularly Alfred Kuby, "Zur Konzeption des Markus-Evangeliums," ZNW 49 (1958): 52–64; Joseph Tyson, "The Blindness of the Disciples in Mark," JBL 80 (1961): 261–68. On theios-aner christology and suffering christology, see n. 5 (for a defini-tion of theios-aner christology see below p. 55). On structural analysis of the Gospel, cf. Eduard Schweizer, "Die theologische Leistung des Markus," EvTh 24 (1964): 337–55, and idem, "Mark's Contribution to the Quest of the Historical Jesus," NTS 10 (1964): 421–32; Leander Keck, "The Introduction to Mark's Gospel," NTS 12 (1966): 341 ff.; Norman Perrin, "Towards an Interpretation of the Gospel of Mark," an unpublished paper; and Robin Scroggs, "Mark: Theologian of the Incarna-tion," an unpublished paper presented to the Society of Biblical Literature, New York, 1970.

12. It is not at all obvious that by beginning with the theory of the messianic secret one shall understand the evangelist's theology and pur-pose any better than if one pursues an investigation of some other redac-tional emphasis. See Keck, "Introduction," pp. 369–70.

matic model for interpreting the Gospel. From his study
he draws the following conclusions. The Gospel is preaching, not history. It originated in a community in Galilee
anxiously awaiting the parousia. It was composed backwards in order to provide historical and theological continuity between that Galilean community and the Jesus of
Galilee.[13]

Johannes Schreiber also is conceptually guided by
Kähler's thesis but begins his investigation not with the
first pericope but with the crucifixion story. His apparent
logic is that since what precedes the passion narrative is
introduction, the heart of the Gospel lies in Mark's crucifixion account. There he finds two traditions wedded by
the evangelist to his own perspective, which, according
to Schreiber, turns out to be a belief that the crucifixion
is not a humiliation but exaltation for Jesus. In Schreiber's
reconstruction, the Markan Jesus could pass as a double
for the Johannine Jesus. Jesus' death is his enthronement.
Salvation is present at the cross. Mark is not concerned with
anxious awaiting of the imminent dawn of the parousia,
contrary to Marxsen's thinking. The parousia is for unbelievers. It will make manifest to them the judgment and
salvation already present for the believers in the cross. For
Christians the eschaton is already present in the cross. The
Gospel is written to show that Jesus' life and the believer's
life are guided by the will of God.[14] One can see that
such things as the meaning of chapter 13, geographical
areas (e.g., Galilee), and other phenomena in the Gospel
take on entirely different connotations, depending upon
whether one is guided by the "visible, unified theological
conception" of Marxsen or of Schreiber.

On the other hand, if one follows Quentin Quesnell,
one begins an investigation of Mark at 6:52. This verse
attributes to hardness of heart the disciples' failure to
recognize Jesus walking on the sea and their failure to
understand the meaning of the loaves in the feeding of the

13. Marxsen, *Mark*, pp. 30 ff., 209.
14. Schreiber, *Theologie*, pp. 22 ff., 45 ff., 77 ff., 126 ff., 233–34.

five thousand. The result of Quesnell's beginning his study of Mark at this point is that the whole Gospel is interpreted through this particular verse. Thus, the motif of incomprehension, the concept of mystery (see 4:11–12), and the emphasis on bread in a number of pericopes all point to Mark's message to his reader. That is that the Christian faith is a mystery which can be understood only through faith in the resurrection. It is a mystery symbolically expressed and experientially known in the celebration of the eucharist.

Why Quesnell decides methodologically that one should begin an interpretation of the Gospel at 6:52 rather than any other point is not quite clear. Despite the fact that he offers some extremely fine guidelines for redaction-critical methodology, along with appropriate words of caution in the application of the methodology, he does not help us to know why we should start at 6:52, except that he finds past explanations of the verse unsatisfactory.[15]

Other examples could be cited, but these should suffice to indicate the hermeneutical circles in which one can go around in Markan research. The problem is not that Schreiber's first principle is invalid. The problem is that no one has given us sufficient direction in determining how we should implement it so that its application leads us to the interpretation of the Gospel intended by the evangelist. What is needed is a methodological approach that will guide one in the accurate interpretation of the

15. Quentin Quesnell, *The Mind of Mark*, Analecta Biblica, no. 38 (Rome: Pontifical Biblical Institute, 1969). Quesnell (pp. 46–57) sets up four corollaries for redaction-critical methodology not too unlike Schreiber's principles: (1) Markan investigation must stick to the extant text, (2) Markan study must keep in mind the author's intended meaning in the text and how the intended audience would have responded to it, (3) the key to understanding is found in redactional elements, and (4) the norm of interpretation should be that the composition has a basic intelligible unity. Quesnell advises that redaction criticism be practiced with caution because (1) we do not know the exact audience Mark addressed, where he lived, or what his relation to his audience was; (2) since redaction is a continuous process, there is the probability of "innumerable layers of redaction in a gospel text"; and (3) we do not know the degree of mastery Mark had over his material or what may have been interpolated at a later date after Mark.

data amassed from analytical study of the Gospel, and that will help safeguard one from the hermeneutical snare of reading into the Gospel preconceived ideas that do violence to the author's intent. Without such a guideline, depending on how one wishes to read the evidence, one critical interpretation may be as convincing as another.

I wish now to introduce such a methodological approach, fully aware that there is no such thing as a foolproof answer to the problem of the hermeneutical circles which plagues Markan research. I believe the application of the following methodological procedure will enable us to discover, with the aid of Schreiber's methodological principles, the evangelist's original purpose in writing.

The only way to interpret the Gospel as the author intended it is to read his work with the analytical eyes of a first century reader. That means in some way assuming the conceptual and analytical stance of a reader in the first century, a solution that is easier stated than implemented. (We cannot ignore the fact that we are historically and culturally bound by our own life situation.) We cannot take a time-machine journey back to the first century. Even if we could, we would still tend to think in the categories of the twentieth century mind-set rather than in the thought patterns of the first century. Yet this should not deter us from trying to approximate as closely as possible the stance which the first century reader might have taken toward the Gospel.

To put ourselves within the first reader's frame of reference we must rid ourselves of any preconceived notions that he would not have brought to his reading of Mark. First, there is no evidence that the first century reader would have recognized the Gospel as either a passion narrative or a resurrection story (Hamilton)[16] with a long introduction. Second, I am not convinced that the first reader would have perceived that the hermeneutical presupposition for the Gospel genre is the messianic secret.

16. Neill Q. Hamilton, *Jesus for a No-God World* (Philadelphia: Westminster Press, 1969), pp. 56–68.

To press further, there is no way of knowing how much knowledge of the kerygma the first reader brought to his reading of Mark. It is extremely doubtful that he possessed an extended narrative about Jesus, such as one finds in Mark, before the Gospel came into his hands. He certainly did not possess the more "complete" documents of Matthew, Luke, and John against which to compare the strengths and weaknesses of Mark. Consequently, he would not have known that the document he was reading was not a "complete" Gospel and that its author had shortchanged him on the teachings of Jesus and other data. He could not have said with the confidence of some contemporary exegetes that the absence of resurrection appearances proves that someone tampered with this manuscript. How would he have known that all other Gospels close with both the empty-tomb story and resurrection appearances, confirming the fact that the conclusion to this manuscript had been "lost"? We can align ourselves more closely with the interpretive perspective of the first reader of Mark only by freeing ourselves of such assumptions and prejudices brought to the Gospel as a result of our previous historical-critical research.

Up to this point I have argued that in order to prepare oneself to respond like a first century reader, one must disengage himself from certain preconceived notions of the twentieth century mind-set, a process which is purgative. But is there a positive frame of reference which one can adopt that places one in the thought patterns of a reader in the first century? I believe there is.

The best way to begin thinking like a first century reader is to be guided by the same principles and procedures of literary analysis that he was. According to H. I. Marrou, in his book *A History of Education in Antiquity*, Greek and Roman education in the century before and in the first centuries of the Christian era focused on pedantic study of the great literary works of the past.[17] The center

17. H. I. Marrou, *A History of Education in Antiquity*, trans. George Lamb (New York: Sheed and Ward, 1956). What follows is a condensation of his discussion on pp. 160–70; 277–81.

of attention in the primary and secondary stages of Greek education belonged to the epic poets, particularly Homer, and the tragedians, especially Euripides, Aeschylus, and Sophocles. Not drawing the same amount of attention but highly revered were the prose writers Herodotus, Xenophon, Hellanicus, and particularly Thucydides. Education in this period was marked by an insatiable curiosity in the classroom to know all that could be learned, to even the most minute detail, about the works of these literary artists of the golden age of Greek literature.

The methodological procedure for the study of these works involved the following steps. Before placing a work in a student's hands the teacher gave the class a summary of the work, apparently using graphic techniques, such as pictures hung on the walls and bas-reliefs, to annotate dramatically the important characters and events. The story having been thus etched on the student's mind, the teacher then placed the critical text in the hands of the student and guided him in "expressive reading" of the work. In all likelihood the procedure in the case of plays and epics consisted of reading the text in dialogue with other students. Once the content had become quite familiar, attention was turned to interpretation of the work. This step encompassed a careful investigation of the vocabulary, the careful noting of terms peculiar to an author, a study of morphology, and a meticulous investigation of characters and events.

Interest in characters was particularly pronounced. There seems to have been a preoccupation with knowing all there was to know about the characters portrayed by the masters, and students were apparently tested to see how well they had committed to memory the facts about these characters. Indicative of this is the catechetical drill of questions of Dionysius Thrax, a noted grammarian of the period. As ludicrous as it may appear to the modern reader, this interest in character study concerned itself even with such trivia as "to know that Heracles was bald when he came out of the seamonster which had swallowed him for a moment when he was trying to rescue Hesione from it."

While this preoccupation with the minutia of characterization strikes a modern student as an absurd and wasteful exercise in pedantry, for the Hellenistic student the command of such information was the sign of a well-educated person.

The final step in a Greek student's investigation of a literary work was "judgment." This involved extrapolating some moral principle from the thoughts and behavior of the characters. The fact that the author might not have intended such moralization appears not to have been considered by Hellenistic grammarians. It was their assumption that the heroes of ancient works served as models for human virtue and vice. Plutarch is representative of the hermeneutical approach advocated. In his work "On the Way in Which Young Men Should Read the Poets," for instance, he instructs his reader that the purpose of Homer's description of Paris forsaking his battlefield for the bed of Helen is to paint in bold strokes his condemnation of such behavior.

This approach to literary analysis in Greek primary and secondary education was universally applied in the Hellenistic world. In Roman education the authors studied were often Roman rather than Greek, but the methodology for elucidating a text was a mimicry of the Greek procedure. In fact, the Roman grammarians appear to have been more interested in an erudite study of characters and events than were the Greeks. One is certainly struck by the way in which Hellenistic education sought to understand the purpose of a work and the mind of the writer through the characters[18] and the events which engulfed them.

This emphasis on characterization as the medium through which an author expresses his message was not, however, confined only to interpretive reading of ancient authors. The cardinal tenets for literary interpretation were similarly the

18. When I refer to character portrayal, I do not have in mind character study in the modern sense but rather presentation of characters as a medium through which an ancient author dramatizes the theses of his composition.

cardinal principles which guided literary creativity. One
wrote the way one thought the ancient writers had written.
This is particularly true of the Hellenistic historian. As
early as the fourth century B.C. Greek historians had begun
to forsake the principles of historiography followed by
Herodotus and Thucydides. They wrote history not so much
in the interest of accurate information as in the interest of
guiding the reader to a moralistic interpretation of the
world. In this way history was used to inspire him to
emulate the lives of the virtuous and to disdain the lives
of the corrupt. Thus the model for writing history during
the Hellenistic period became the Greek drama, and the
vehicle for eliciting such moralistic judgments from the
reader became characterization.[19]

Perhaps there is no better illustration of such an interpretation of history than that of the Roman historian Livy
(59 B.C.–A.D. 17). Livy's view that the meaning of history
is best seen in the people who act it out is well attested
by the remarks addressed to his reader in the preface to
his *Ab Urbe Condita* ("The History of Rome"):

> Here are the questions to which I would have every reader
> give his close attention—what life and morals were like; through
> what men and by what policies, in peace and war, empire was
> established and enlarged; then let him note how . . . morals first
> gave way . . . sank lower and lower, and finally began the down-
> ward plunge which has brought us to the present time. . . . What
> chiefly makes the study of history wholesome and profitable is
> this, that you behold the lessons of every kind of experience set
> forth as on a conspicuous monument; from these you may choose
> for yourself and for your own state what to imitate, from these
> mark for avoidance what is shameful in the conception and shame-
> ful in the result.[20]

In drawing out this meaning of history through his
characters, Livy rarely offers direct personal commentary
on the ramifications of their lives. He chooses, rather, to

---

19. See P. G. Walsh, *Livy: His Historical Aims and Methods* (London:
Cambridge Press, 1961), pp. 21–26.

20. Titus Livius, *Ab Urbe Condita*, trans. B. O. Foster, Loeb Classical
Library (London: William Heinemann, 1919), pp. 5–7.

provide such interpretation indirectly by the way in which he depicts and highlights traits and actions of his characters within the historical drama. In commenting on this practice by Livy, P. G. Walsh notes:

> Instead of making personal observations on the character of individuals, the historian is content to use "indirect" methods which we associate with the medium of drama, so that the reader forms his impression of individuals in three ways. First, the speeches and remarks made by a person give the reader an insight into his character; here the historian, allowed by convention some freedom in the reporting of speeches, has his greatest opportunity to influence our assessment. Secondly, the attitudes of contemporaries towards the person characterised, as expressed in their speeches, are important; here too the historian can subtly introduce rearrangement and change of emphasis. Thirdly, the effect which the person characterised has on other people can be depicted by describing either their mental reactions on encountering him, or the courses they subsequently adopt.[21]

Often the effect which Livy wishes to create for the reader's judgment requires that he take serious liberties with historical personages: reshaping, redirecting, in fact rewriting their lives to meet his own needs. The concern for historical accuracy is set aside. The heroes are idealized. The villains are denigrated. For Livy this is not misrepresentation of history but its proper interpretation.

This quick look at Hellenistic interests in literary analysis and composition supplies us with extremely helpful clues to understand how the first reader might have looked at the Gospel when he first took it up in his hands. As a Hellenistic man able to read the Markan Greek, the first reader must have been guided in his interpretation of Mark by the same procedures applied in Hellenistic education. It matters not how educated a man he was. He would have been introduced to such hermeneutical principles in the very earliest stages of his education. Besides, since no other rhetorical principles than these were taught or applied in Hellenistic education, the Hellenistic reader's or hearer's interpretative stance is fixed by his culture, regardless of the level of his educational achievement.

21. Walsh, *Livy*, pp. 82–83. See also Walsh's description of Livy's method, pp. 82–109.

Further support for the assumption that the first reader would have approached the Gospel guided by the same hermeneutical principles that he used when he read the tragedians or the historians is suggested by the nature of the Gospel genre. Although many scholars have pointed out that the creation of the Gospel is the creation of a new literary genre,[22] it nevertheless approximates the style of the Greek drama and the popular lives of the time; there is every reason to suspect that the reader would have approached the Gospel in much the same way as these other analogous types of literature.[23] He would have perceived that character portrayal and the events in which the major characters are involved are the points of focus from which one understands the message of the Gospel.

But would the author of the Gospel have intended that his reader read the Gospel in this fashion, or assumed that he would? Would the author have written with this in mind? Why not? The evangelist shows no great literary talent. His composition is artless compared to the work of Livy. There is no reason to think that he is attempting to blaze any new paths for literary interpretation or composition. There is no reason to believe that he would not have followed the same literary perspective and techniques of authors of similar compositions in his time.

We ought not to pass up at this point one suggestive comparison between the literary technique of the evangelist and his contemporaries. In our discussion of Livy it was

22. For comprehensive studies comparing the Gospel genre with other literary types, see C. W. Votaw, "The Gospels and Contemporary Biographies," *AJT* 19 (1915): 45–73, 217–49; K. L. Schmidt, "Die Stellung der Evangelien in der allgemeinen Literaturgeschichte," ΕΥΧΑΡΙΣΤΗΡΙΟΝ, ed. H. Schmidt (Göttingen: Vandenhoeck and Ruprecht, 1923), 2:50–134. See also Rudolf Bultmann, *History of the Synoptic Tradition*, trans. John Marsh (Oxford: Basil Blackwell, 1963), pp. 368–74; Martin Dibelius, *From Tradition to Gospel*, trans. B. L. Woolf (New York: Charles Scribner's Sons, 1935), pp. 39–40; M. L. Hadas and Morton Smith, *Heroes and Gods* (New York: Harper & Row, 1965).

23. See Votaw, "The Gospels," pp. 45–73, 217–49; Ernest W. Burch, "Tragic Action in the Second Gospel: A Study in the Narrative of Mark," *JR* 11 (1931): 346–58; D. W. Riddle, *The Gospels: Their Origin and Growth* (Chicago: University of Chicago Press, 1939), pp. 141 ff.; Dan Via, Jr., *The Parables: Their Literary and Existential Dimension* (Philadelphia: Fortress Press, 1967), pp. 179 ff.

noted that he seldom makes direct personal comment on
the lives of people about whom he narrates. Rather, he
comments indirectly by the way in which he portrays the
actions and thoughts of the personages in his historical
drama. Scholars have often pondered over the fact that
Mark never comments personally or expresses himself directly to the reader (with the possible exception of 13:14).
Might he not choose, as Livy did, to comment indirectly
to his readers by the way he portrays his characters and
the events in which they participate?

Thus we are on fairly safe ground in assuming that the
first reader would have instinctively turned to the Markan
characters, their portrayal, and the events which engulfed
them as the starting point for understanding the composition. From careful reflection upon the attitudes, speeches,
and behavior of these characters he would have extrap-
olated insights which would have guided him in understanding the intention and message of the writer. He would
have taken this approach not only because he would have
known no other way to proceed in interpreting this type
of literature but also because the author likewise would have
intended and assumed such an approach. Thus there is
no question as to where a twentieth century reader should
begin in his understanding of the Gospel, if he wishes to
understand it in a manner in any way approximating that
in which his first century predecessor read it. The twentieth
century reader must start with the Markan characters. They
hold the key to the mystery surrounding the creation of
the Gospel.[24]

24. This same general approach to the investigation of characters in a
Gospel drama has been followed most recently by J. Louis Martyn in
his interpretation of the Gospel of John, *History and Theology in the
Fourth Gospel* (New York: Harper & Row, 1969). See also T. W. Manson,
The Teaching of Jesus (London: Cambridge University Press, 1945), and
J. Arthur Baird, *Audience Criticism and the Historical Jesus* (Philadelphia:
Westminster Press, 1969), who also find the personae in the Gospel drama
important but for different reasons. Their interest is to recover the authen-
tic teachings of Jesus through what Baird calls audience criticism. Robert
P. Meye, *Jesus and the Twelve* (Grand Rapids, Mich.: William B. Eerd-

Thanks to a knowledge of Hellenistic literary hermeneutics we have found common ground with the first reader of Mark. We can begin at approximately the same point at which he began in interpreting the Gospel. Unfortunately, a common starting point and projected analytical direction is all that we do share with the first century reader. From that point on we must go our different ways in arriving at an understanding of Mark. He begins with his hermeneutical approach and draws conclusions about the implications of Mark from what he already knows of the situation that prompted the writing. We are not privileged to such foreknowledge. We must begin with the same hermeneutical approach and then reconstruct that situation with data gathered through careful critical analysis. Yet, though we would also wish to take the same path as our first century predecessor, at least we share a common compass setting. It is hoped that this compass setting will help us chart and guide our course so that the conclusion we reach is not unlike that which our first reader reached.

---

mans Publishing Co., 1968), pp. 90 ff., recognizes, too, the importance of characters (specifically the disciples) for the community reading Mark.

Quesnell, *Mark,* p. 47, comes very close to the same methodological interest that I am suggesting in what he argues: "A reaction to and understanding of the text which would be normal and expected in the milieu of the audience for whom the text was written is a probable or certain key to the meaning of the text, when that audience, milieu, and likely reaction are known with probability or certitude."

Quesnell apparently has failed to see the important application of his profound insight in terms of the particular ways in which any reader in the Hellenistic environment would have read Mark. He thinks solely in terms of a specific audience identified by specialized interests.

I

Key Characters in the Markan Drama

The major Markan characters or groups of characters are the religious "Establishment," the ubiquitous crowds, the disciples, and Jesus. These figures enter and exit with recurring regularity from the beginning to the end of the Markan drama. Other personae such as John the Baptist, Pilate, and the Galilean women play significant roles. Their exposure on stage, however, is minimal compared to that of the major figures. If the key to Mark's intent lies in his characterization, then these major characters offer the most likely place to find that key.

It certainly requires no burst of insight to recognize that the members of the religious Establishment[1] in Mark function as the enemies of Jesus and are responsible for the untimely and unnatural end of his life. To be sure, the intensity and scope of the Jewish authorities' opposition to Jesus does not originate with Mark, nor can it be said that it reflects accurately the original animus which existed between the religious Establishment and the man from Nazareth. Already before Mark the early church had turned this original enmity to its own purpose, altering and expanding upon it to suit the church's own needs in addressing itself to the bitter controversies that characterized Jewish opposition to Christianity in the first three decades of the church. Yet at the same time Mark's own insertion of references to the "Establishment" throughout his narrative[2] and his position-

1. Members by party: Pharisees and Sadducees; by office: scribes, elders, chief priests. See Joachim Jeremias, *Jerusalem in the Time of Jesus*, trans. F. H. Cave and C. H. Cave (Philadelphia: Fortress Press, 1969) for an excellent study of these parties and figures.

2. Redactional passages where references to the authorities are found are 1:22; 2:6, 16, 18; 3:6, 22; 7:1; 8:11; 9:14; 11:18; 12:13, 28; 14:1. See Rudolf Bultmann, *History of the Synoptic Tradition*, trans. John Marsh (Oxford: Basil Blackwell, 1963), on respective passages and Étienne Trocmé, *La Formation de l'Évangile selon Marc* (Paris: Presses Universitaires de France, 1963), pp. 73 ff.

ing of the material he received on the Jewish hierarchy's antipathy toward Jesus produces such dramatic tension and movement that the hostility existing between Jesus and the authorities reflected in the Gospel must be laid to more than Mark's dispassionate passing on of tradition.

Our evangelist's staging of the conflict between Jesus and the religious leaders begins at the outset of Jesus' ministry (1:22). With rhythmic regularity and accelerated intensity the conflict is flashed before the eyes of the reader,[3] reaching crescendos of dramatic moment at 3:6; 8:31; 9:31; 10:33; 11:18; 12:12, and culminating in the final climactic event: the death of Jesus by the insidious design of the Jewish authorities (15:1–39).

Étienne Trocmé interprets this Markan staging as a polemic against a Jewish-Christian group in the evangelist's community which seeks a rapprochement with Judaism in matters relating to ritual purity, eschatology, and exorcism.[4] There is a polemical thrust in Mark against certain Jewish practices. But to read into this attack a programmatic assault upon the Jewish religious Establishment in the Jerusalem of Mark's day and an assault upon the mother church at Jerusalem is not warranted. Jesus' sanctioning of priestly practice at 1:44 and occasional advocacy of Mosaic teaching (7:10–13; 10:17–19; 12:28–34) and Mark's setting of Jesus' ministry in the synagogue speaks against a thoroughgoing Jewish polemic.[5] I find it difficult to argue more than that the evangelist's characterization of the Jewish hierarchy serves to establish in the reader's mind that Jesus' death was a tragic result of the hierarchy's insidious reaction to Jesus' ministry and his popularity with the masses.[6]

---

3. Mark 2:6 ff., 16 ff., 24 ff.; 3:1 ff., 22 ff.; 7:1 ff.; 8:11 ff., 15; 10:1 ff.; 11:15 ff., 27–33; 12:1–38; 14:1–2, 10–11, 43–65.

4. Trocmé *La Formation,* pp. 70–95. See also somewhat similarly Siegfried Schulz, "Markus und das Alte Testament," *ZTK* 58 (1961): 185–97.

5. Cf. Leander Keck, "Mark 3:7–12 and Mark's Christology," *JBL* 84 (1965): 344, and T. A. Burkill, *Mysterious Revelation* (Ithaca, N. Y.: Cornell University Press, 1963), pp. 37 ff.

6. E.g., 1:22, 27; 2:6–12; 3:19b–22; 11:18; 12:12, 37b–40; 14:1–2; 15:10.

The second ubiquitous group of characters to concern us are the nondescript masses. The fact that this amorphous gathering of humanity emerges time and time again throughout the Gospel drama and the fact that the terms used to identify it are often found in redactional passages[7] suggest that the ubiquitous crowd has a special role in the drama. That role is to dramatize, by contrast with the religious leaders, the positive response to Jesus. The crowds flock to him with eagerness (1:32 ff., 37; 3:7–12; 4:1; 6:53–56; 9:15; 11:8 ff.), listen to his teaching enthusiastically (1:22, 27; 12:37b), and respond to his healing powers with anticipation (1:32 ff.; 3:7 ff.; 6:53 ff.).

Unlike Robinson I do not believe that the masses are cast in a derogatory manner, as an obstacle to Jesus' ministry.[8] It is true that the crowd appears to get in Jesus' way (2:4; 3:20; 5:31[?]). But this is a literary device to dramatize the popularity of Jesus with the masses, and it serves well the evangelist's schema of starkly contrasting the populace's acclaim of Jesus with the bitterly hostile reaction of the Jewish hierarchy.[9] That this schematic contrast is at the center

7. Identified usually by the terms *crowd* (thirty-seven times), the undefined *they* (e.g., 1:22, 32, 45), *many* (2:2, 15; 6:2, 31, 33; 10:48; 11:8), *all* (1:27; 2:12; 5:20), *multitude* (3:7, 8), and *people* (14:2). A number of references to the masses undoubtedly belonged to Mark's sources (e.g., 1:27; 2:4; 5:24, 27, 30, 31; 8:6) but note the redactional instances at 2:13; 3:7–9, 20; 4:1; 5:20, 21; 6:31, 45; 7:14, 17; 9:14–15; 10:1, 46; 11:18; 12:12, 37. On the redactional character of these verses and the Markan use of the crowds, cf. Bultmann, *History,* pp. 342–43; Robert P. Meye, *Jesus and the Twelve* (Grand Rapids, Mich.: William B. Eerdmans Publishing Co., 1968), pp. 118 ff.; and Eduard Schweizer, *The Good News According to Mark,* trans. D. H. Madvig (Richmond, Va.: John Knox Press, 1970).

8. James M. Robinson, "The Problem of History in Mark, Reconsidered," *USQR* 20 (1965): 71 ff.

9. See Schweizer, *The Good News,* pp. 242, 287. Mark 5:17; 6:2 ff.; 14:43; 15:11 represent the few places where the populace responds negatively to Jesus. Mark 5:17, probably a part of the original story, highlights the miraculous powers of Jesus rather than disdain of him. Mark 6:2 ff. in all probability is a vestige of an antifamily polemic (see 3:31–35; cf. Trocmé, *La Formation,* pp. 107 ff.). Mark 14:43 is a narrower use of the term *crowd* in referring to a special group representing the religious authorities. The chief priests are responsible for inciting the crowd to reject Jesus in 15:11 ff.

of the author's thought is certainly underscored by the number of instances in which he highlights this contrast of reaction to Jesus by lacing such extreme responses back to back (e.g., 2:6–12; 3:1–12, 19b–22; 6:53–7:13; 10:1–16; 11:8–18; 12:12; 14:1–2).

The Markan Portrayal of the Disciples

Aside from Jesus, the character-group which monopolizes Mark's attention most is the disciples, specifically the Twelve. It is hardly necessary in the present stage of Markan research to state that Mark has a particular interest in the Twelve.[10] Why he has such an interest is a hotly debated question. At first glance one might be prompted to suggest that just as the Establishment-group is portrayed as the enemies of Jesus and the mass-group as his acclaimants, so quite naturally the disciples-group serves to dramatize the nature of proper discipleship. But such a conclusion would be drawn too hastily. For while the Establishment-group and mass-group are drawn rather simply in a one-dimensional fashion—their position is quite clear—the role of the disciples in Mark is far more intricately developed and far more difficult to interpret. Because of their special intimate association with Jesus—an association initiated by Jesus—in which the disciples are made the special agents for the extension of his ministry (3:13–19; 6:7), the receivers of special revelation (e.g., 4:10 ff., 34; 9:30–31; 13:1 ff.), and his confidants (14:32 ff.), one is at times tempted to argue that they are his closest and most responsive friends and trusted companions. At other times, because of their obstinacy (e.g., 4:13; 6:51–52; 8:14–21; 9:32) and rejection of Jesus (14:10, 50, 66–71), one is led to believe that the disciples belong with the religious Establishment as enemies of Jesus.

10. Cf. Bultmann, *History*, pp. 343 ff.; Trocmé, *La Formation*, p. 128; Erich Grässer, "Jesus in Nazareth, (Mark VI. 1–6a)," *NTS* 16 (1969): 10; Meye, *Jesus*, pp. 93 ff.

This ambivalent behavior of the disciples has puzzled and intrigued scholars for some time. Though the disciples are the carefully picked confidants of Jesus, heroes of the early church, authorities for authentic christology and discipleship, ironically they emerge in the Markan drama with extremely poor performances both in terms of their perspicacity about Jesus' teaching and ministry and in terms of their loyalty to him. Some nineteenth and twentieth century scholars who argued that Mark was an objective historian recounting the reminiscences of Peter viewed these disappointing performances as historically accurate accounts of the disciples' behavior which Peter confessionally reported. Since William Wrede, others have interpreted the poor performances of the disciples in Mark as a by-product of the evangelist's overarching theological motif, the messianic secret, in which case the evangelist's purpose has been viewed not as an attempt to berate the disciples but rather as an attempt to point up and clarify better the phenomenon of the Christ-event.[11] In both points of view whatever unfavorable picture of the disciples the evangelist may have produced has not been interpreted as the evangelist's attempt to bring dishonor upon them. Rather it has been interpreted either as his candid statement of the facts of tradition or as the inevitable consequences of the development of the messianic secret. It has generally been believed that, where such unfavorable pictures of the disciples do occur in the Gospel, the evangelist and his readers would have drawn upon the glorified and highly esteemed post-resurrection image of the disciples to counteract any momentary misapprehensions about their venerableness. In this way, it was assumed, both the evangelist and his readers

---

11. William Wrede, *Das Messiasgeheimnis in den Evangelien*, 3d ed. (Göttingen: Vandenhoeck and Ruprecht, 1963). Cf. also H. J. Ebeling, *Das Messiasgeheimnis und die Botschaft des Marcus-Evangelisten* (Berlin: Alfred Töpelmann, 1939), and Erik Sjöberg, *Der verborgene Menschensohn in den Evangelien* (Lund, Sweden: C. W. K. Gleerup, 1955), who are indebted to Wrede's insights, but arrive at different understandings of the origin or purpose of the secret. See David E. Aune, "The Problem of the Messianic Secret, *Nov Test* 11 (1969): 1–31 for the influence of Wrede's position.

would have understood that the Gospel was not intended to bring any real dishonor to the memory of the disciples, no matter how disgraced they may look in different episodes of Jesus' life.[12]

What all these scholars have refused to consider is the possibility that these Markan episodes in which the disciples are placed in such an unfavorable light may be more than just the result of the passing on of a tradition or the consequence of the development of a theological motif to set off the greatness of the Christ-event. They have failed to consider seriously the possibility that the evangelist might be attacking the disciples intentionally, for whatever reason. A good example of this hermeneutical intransigence is the position of A. E. J. Rawlinson. On one occasion a friend of his remarked, "How Mark does hate the Twelve!" Rawlinson replied, "The remark betrayed, no doubt, an exaggerated impression; the Twelve are certainly not spared in this Gospel, but it would be a mistake to regard Mark as cherishing any animus against them."[13]

Two Markan exegetes, Johannes Schreiber and Joseph Tyson, have performed an invaluable service for Markan scholarship by freeing it from slavish adherence to classical and pietistic interpretations of the Markan portrayal of the disciples and opening up a fresh, new way to view the Markan treatment of the disciples. Although disagreeing on certain particulars, they both have argued that Mark's portrayal of the disciples must be seen as a literary device in the service of a polemic against a conservative Jewish Christian group in Palestine which placed no positive meaning in Jesus' death, held to the long-established Jewish practices, and rejected the necessity of the gentile mission.

---

12. See Wrede, *Messiasgeheimnis*, pp. 106–13; Sjöberg, *Der . . . Menschensohn*, pp. 127 ff.; recently, Burkill, *Mysterious Revelation*, pp. 168–87; Ulrich Luz, "Das Geheimnismotiv und die Markanische Christologie," *ZNW* 55 (1965): 26; Meye, *Jesus*, p. 85; Quentin Quesnell, *The Mind of Mark*, Analecta Biblica, no. 38 (Rome: Pontifical Biblical Institute, 1969), p. 170.

13. A. E. J. Rawlinson, *St. Mark* (London: Methuen and Co., 1925), p. xxviii.

One of the reasons Mark wrote his Gospel was to attack the position of this reactionary group and its leaders (Tyson: the family of Jesus; Schreiber: Peter, James, and John), who are represented by the disciples in the Gospel drama.[14] I am convinced, with Tyson and Schreiber, that a careful analysis of Mark's presentation of the disciples supports the contention that Mark is engaged in a polemic against the disciples, though not a polemic of the same character which Tyson and Schreiber outline.[15]

Three Stages in the Disciples' Relationship to Jesus

Stage I: Unperceptiveness

I believe that it is possible to detect in Mark three successive and progressively worsening stages in the relation between Jesus and the disciples.[16] The first such stage occurs in the first half of the Gospel (1:16–8:26) and is characterized by the disciples' inability to perceive who Jesus is. Despite the continuous manifestation of Jesus' messiahship before the disciples in countless healings,[17] exorcisms,[18] and

14. Johannes Schreiber, "Die Christologie des Markusevangeliums," *ZTK* 58 (1961): 175–83; idem, *Theologie des Vertrauens* (Hamburg: Furche-Verlag H. Rennebach K. G., 1967), pp. 101–n, 112 ff., 127–29, 165 ff.; Joseph Tyson, "The Blindness of the Disciples in Mark," *JBL* 80 (1961): 261–68.

15. The points at which I disagree with Tyson and Schreiber will become obvious in subsequent discussions. See Keck, "Mark's Christology," pp. 356 ff. for well-founded criticisms of Schreiber.

16. I am much indebted to Alfred Kuby's article ("Zur Konzeption des Markus-Evangeliums," *ZNW* 49 [1958]: 52–64) for insights into Mark's schematic presentation of the disciples' relation with Jesus; however, I find, as the following discussion will show, that the evidence calls for diagraming and interpreting the Markan presentation of the disciples somewhat differently from Kuby's two stages (1:16–8:21 and 8:22 ff.). Somewhat similar to Kuby are the recent studies by Meye, *Jesus*, pp. 63–85, and particularly the redaction-critical study of Quesnell, *Mark*, pp. 58–176, on Mark's use of the nonunderstanding motif in his portrayal of the relation of Jesus to the disciples.

17. Mark 1:29–31, 32–34, 40–45; 2:1–12; 3:1–5, 9–10; 5:21–43; 6:1–6, 53–56; 7:31–37; 8:22–26.

18. Mark 1:21–28, 32–34, 39; 3:11; 5:1–20; 7:24–30.

nature miracles,[19] they remain amazingly obtuse and obdurate in the face of their involvement in the messianic drama. Not even in their own miraculous activity, to which they are commissioned (3:15; 6:7) and in which they are successful (6:13), do the disciples appear to detect their relationship to Jesus and his true identity. In fact, this amazing and unbelievable lack of perception by the disciples, appears to increase rather than to diminish and becomes more persistent as the narrative unfolds (1:37; 4:10, 13, 38–41; 5:31; 6:37, 51–52; 7:17; 8:4, 14–21). It is particularly astonishing when one realizes that throughout Mark the disciples enjoy a special and privileged position before Jesus which is open to no one else. They are a select and exclusive group of intimate associates (1:16–20; 3:13 ff.), commissioned to convey his message and continue his ministry (3:14–15; 6:7–13), entrusted with secret instruction (4:11–12, 33–34; 9:30–31), and occasionally appointed as his assistants in the performance of miraculous acts (6:37–43; 8:1–10).

Yet ironically those far less well acquainted with Jesus appear to respond to him with far greater insights than do the disciples. This is not to say that the "outsiders" (4:11) recognized Jesus as the Messiah, but they at least saw in Jesus the powers and qualities of a great miracle worker.[20] The disciples, despite Jesus' having empowered them to perform miraculous acts (3:14–15; 6:7) and their resulting success with such acts (6:13), show an inexplicable inability to recognize Jesus' miraculous power. To illustrate: as Alfred Kuby has pointed out, in the stilling of the storm (4:35–41) the disciples do not call out for Jesus to intercede with a supernatural act but rather are dismayed that Jesus does not seem to be concerned about their plight. They exhibit no faith in Jesus as one who can save them (4:40).[21]

19. Mark 4:35–41; 6:35–44, 45–52; 8:1–10.

20. Mark 1:32–34, 35–38, 40–45; 2:1–12; 3:7–12; 5:1–20, 21–43; 6:53–56; 7:24–30; 8:22–26.

21. Kuby, "Zur Konzeption," p. 56. See Bornkamm in Günther Bornkamm, Gerhard Barth, and H. J. Held, *Tradition and Interpretation in Matthew*, trans. Percy Scott (Philadelphia: Westminster Press, 1963), pp. 53 ff.

Similarly, in Mark 5:25 ff. the woman with the hemorrhage recognizes at first sight healing powers in Jesus which no other physician has—powers so great that even by touching his garments one can be healed (5:28–29). But the disciples, who have accompanied Jesus through all his miraculous ministry, are unaware of this power (5:30–31) and respond uncomprehendingly to Jesus' discovery that someone has touched his garment to be healed. As soon as Jesus lands at Gennesaret, people flock to him to be healed (6:53 ff.). They recognize him (vv. 54–55) because of his miraculous powers. Even a Greek (7:24–30) recognizes in Jesus the power of the exorcist. Inexplicably, the disciples, in contrast to this response by "outsiders," are bewildered in 8:4 as to how Jesus will feed four thousand people in the desert, even though he has fed five thousand people by the miraculous multiplication of loaves and fishes. And then, almost immediately after the feeding of the four thousand, the disciples are apprehensive over how they are going to subsist on one loaf of bread during their boat journey, despite the fact that Jesus has by that time clearly demonstrated that he can satisfy the hunger of nine thousand with just a few loaves and fishes (8:14–21). For some strange reason, while others swarm to Jesus as a miracle worker, the disciples are oblivious to Jesus' miraculous power.

This peculiarly Markan presentation of the unperceptiveness of the disciples (1:16–8:26) stands out even more sharply when one compares the Matthean and Lucan treatment of Markan material in which the disciples are pictured as either obtuse, obdurate, or inept. In practically every instance Matthew either omits or alters the Markan passages in question in favor of a better picture of the disciples' acumen. Whereas in Mark 1:37 Peter and the others seek to divert Jesus from his overall purpose (1:38), Matthew deletes the verse, thereby removing any question about the disciples being out of harmony with Jesus' plans or failing to understand his mission. Where the disciples are depicted in Mark 4:13 as incapable of understanding the parable of the sower, when supposedly they are the possessors of the secret meaning of Jesus' teachings (4:11), Matthew deletes the uncomplimentary insinuation. In fact in Matthew's re-writing of the episode the focus of attention is not the disciples' ability or inability to understand parables (so Mark 4:10, 13) but Jesus' purpose in addressing the multitudes in parables (Matt. 13:10).

In Mark 4:38–41 the disciples fail to recognize in Jesus the supernatural help which can save them from the perils of a raging sea, but in the Matthean parallel the cry of the disciples suggests that it is precisely this supernatural help for which the disciples appeal (8:25).[22] Similarly, the disciples' misunderstanding and bold reproof of Jesus in Mark 6:37, when Jesus commands the disciples to feed the hungry multitudes, is all but expurgated in Matthew's recasting of the Markan passage.[23] And in the Matthean parallel to Mark 6:51–52, instead of depicting the disciples as obdurate, Matthew makes the response of the disciples a confessional expression of recognition and worship: "Truly you are the Son of God." (14:33).

While in the Matthean parallels to Mark 7:17–18; 8:4, 14–21 Matthew appears to do an about-face and support the Markan position on the cognitive deficiencies of the disciples, these instances are but minor exceptions to the pervasive Matthean pattern. And even in these apparent contradictions Matthew relativizes and temporizes the Markan picture. Gerhard Barth detects Matthew's temporizing of the Markan picture of obtuseness by the evangelist's addition of the word *still* (Matt. 15:16) to Mark 7:17.[24] In the case of Mark 8:4, the Matthean response of the disciples to Jesus' concern about the hungry four thousand is substantially different. In the Matthean version the disciples interpret Jesus' concern about feeding the multitude as a request for *them* to provide the sustenance. For Matthew the point of the disciples' query is not the disciples' failure

22. Bornkamm, Barth, Held, *Tradition*, pp. 55–56.

23. Ibid., pp. 182–83.

24. Ibid., p. 114.

to understand the powers of Jesus (so Mark) but their recognition of their own limited powers.[25] Finally, with respect to Mark 8:14–21, Gerhard Barth argues that the Matthean rendering of the Markan passage is not a reversal of his usual correction of an unfavorable Markan presentation of the disciples. The point in Matthew is that the disciples failed to understand an enigmatic word of Jesus (Matt. 16: 5–11), not that they failed to appreciate Jesus' miraculous power.[26] In Matthew 16:12, in contrast to the Markan episode, the disciples finally do understand.

It is not just in the altering and deleting of the Markan text that Matthew removes the Markan tarnish from the disciples' image. He also inserts additional material from other sources to restore the revered stature of the disciples. Between Mark 4:12 and 13 he inserts a special blessing upon the disciples, suggesting that they are privileged to sights and teachings that not only are obscure to outsiders (Mark 4:11; Matt. 13:13) but were not revealed even to the prophets and righteous men of the past (13:16–17). In 13: 51 he interjects a passage attesting to the perspicacity of the disciples. In 10:40–41 he draws upon a source which places the disciples in such a venerated position that whoever receives the disciples in effect receives Jesus himself. In 12:49–50 Matthew rewords Mark 3:34–35 to cite the disciples specifically as the true relatives of Jesus, the obedient doers of the Father's will.[27]

When one turns to Luke, one finds that his response to the Markan denigrated presentation of the disciples prior to the Petrine confession is not unlike that of Matthew. In Mark 1:37, where there is perhaps the first hint that Jesus and the disciples are going to be at odds concerning the understanding and implementation of his mission, Luke has made the multitude, not the disciples, responsible for the attempt to divert Jesus from his purpose (4:42–43). Of

25. H. J. Held in ibid., p. 185.

26. Ibid., p. 114.

27. On the Matthean positive reconstruction of the disciples' image, see Gerhard Barth and H. J. Held in ibid., pp. 106 ff., 250–51.

course, in the Lucan narrative it would be impossible for the disciples to be responsible for such a temptation at this point—they are not introduced to the reader until 5:1 ff. Regardless of the reason, Luke removed the disciples from the Markan passage in question; such a rewriting also removed the Markan hint of possible discord between Jesus and the disciples over the conduct of Jesus' ministry.

Like Matthew, Luke deletes the Markan insinuation (4: 13) that the disciples remain without understanding after Jesus has informed them that they are the possessors of "the secret of the kingdom of God" (Luke 8:9 ff.). Luke alters Mark 4:38 ff. (where the disciples cry out in fear to Jesus, but not with any faith in Jesus' ability to save them) to place the disciples in a more favorable light, indicating that they do possess some measure of faith in Jesus' ability to save them.[28] Following a similar procedure, Luke alters the interchange between Jesus and the disciples in Mark 5:31 in favor of a more sympathetic treatment of the disciples in the scene. In Mark the disciples respond to Jesus' query "Who was it that touched me?" with a curt, if not querulous, rejoinder. But in Luke any suggestion of a petulant tone in the disciples' (or in Luke's case, Peter's) response has been banished from the scene. According to the Lucan version, Peter replies to Jesus' question only after all have in turn denied touching Jesus and then only intervenes to mediate the conflict between Jesus, who claims someone has touched him, and the multitude, who deny that any of them did. Similarly, in the case of Mark 6:37, Luke, like Matthew, considered the disciples' bold reproof of Jesus' directive to feed the multitude to be too strong and unbecoming, and so he rewrites the response to be a more proper answer of a disciple to his Lord (9:13).

The damaging insinuations about the disciples' capacity for discernment in Mark 6:51–52; 7:17–18; 8:4, 14–21 have been deleted in Luke. Of course these particular passages

28. See Hans Conzelmann, *The Theology of St. Luke,* trans. Geoffrey Buswell (New York: Harper & Row, 1961), p. 49, and Kuby, "Zur Konzeption," p. 56.

appear in the large section of Mark (6:45–8:26) which Luke
completely omitted; consequently, one cannot argue that
Luke deleted these verses to save the disciples from the
hands of Mark. But for whatever reason he deleted this
Markan section, it still remains true that by such an omis-
sion the Lucan presentation of the disciples emerges without those particular unfavorable Markan comments. The
only Markan verse in any way unfavorable to the disciples
which Luke does not alter or delete prior to the Petrine
confession is the disciples' inquiry concerning the parable
of the sower (Luke 8:9).

Luke's presentation of a more positive and complimentary image of the disciples does not end with his alteration
or deletion of the unfavorable Markan passages. Much like
Matthew, he draws upon additional material from his
sources which tends to place the disciples in a venerated
position. For example, his substitution of his own "call"
story (Luke 5:1–11) in place of the Markan story (1:16 ff.)
provides an entirely different insight into Peter and his
companions in their initial encounter with Jesus. In Mark
the disciples follow Jesus as a result of his invitation, but
there is no indication of what the nature of the disciples'
response really was. Did they accept his invitation because
they recognized him as a good man, a good teacher? Were
they tired of fishing for fish, or what? In Luke's account it
is clear. Peter has been profoundly moved in a religious experience, confesses his sins, and calls Jesus "Lord" as a result
of the miraculous catch (5:8–9). Similarly, Luke paints in
another positive glimpse of the disciples when in the introduction of the Q beatitudes he has Jesus address the blessings specifically to the disciples (6:20 ff.).

Stage II: Misconception

The second stage of the disciples' relation to Jesus is inaugurated in Mark 8:27 ff. With the episode at Caesarea
Philippi (8:27–33) a sudden change takes place in Mark's
rendering of the disciples' capacity for discernment. Peter
experiences a startling revelation: Jesus is the Christ (8:29).

This sudden burst of insight is as inexplicable as the previous unperceptiveness. In 8:21 the disciples appear just as dense and totally unenlightened as they were in the earlier portions of the Gospel. Up to 8:29 there is no indication that they had understood or discovered any of the capabilities of Jesus which even others had discerned. Yet in 8:29 Peter, the spokesman for the disciples, suddenly makes a confession which suggests that the disciples are now as keenly perceptive as they were thoroughly lacking in perception before. Furthermore, this confession encompasses a far greater understanding of Jesus than has been intuited by anyone previously, other than the exorcised demons that Jesus silenced. Previously the greatest insight into the identity of Jesus had been to recognize in him the power of a great miracle worker, or to identify him as John the Baptist redivivus, as Elijah, or as another prophet (6:14–16; 8:27–28). But now Peter has disclosed the ultimate insight: Jesus is the Christ.

Any assumption, however, that by this confession the disciples have received a complete understanding of Jesus is soon proved false by the presentation of the disciples in the subsequent chapters. What was before a period of unperceptiveness has now shifted to a period of misconception. For with the interchange between Peter and Jesus after the confession (8:30–33) it now becomes evident that, while identifying Jesus as the Christ, the disciples do not have the same understanding of the nature of messiahship as Jesus claims for himself. Whatever Peter's concept of messiahship is, it is not Jesus' concept. For Jesus, messiahship can be defined only in terms of suffering and death. Despite his attempts to spell out clearly the path of authentic messiahship (8:31; 9:31; 10:33–34) and the heavenly voice's confirmation of it (9:7),[29] the disciples neither understand (9:32) nor accept this concept of a suffering

29. In 9:7 the heavenly voice seeks to cause the three disciples to abandon their own erroneous concept of what constitutes messiahship and to listen to Jesus; so, Schreiber, *Theologie*, p. 120; Neill Q. Hamilton, *Jesus for a No-God World* (Philadelphia: Westminster Press, 1969), pp. 47–48; and Schweizer, *The Good News*, p. 182.

Messiah (8:32). Consequently, throughout the rest of the
Gospel one finds the disciples and Jesus locked in a continuous conflict over the characteristics of authentic messiahship
and the commitment to suffering discipleship which is de-
manded of the disciples of a suffering Messiah. It is a
christological conflict that is never resolved. Each time Jesus
attempts to explain his position on his christological nature
the disciples either rebuke him (8:31–32) or react in fear
and with a lack of understanding (9:5-6, 10, 32). Or they
indicate their misunderstanding of Jesus by seeking and subscribing to a type of discipleship which stands in diametric
opposition to the type of discipleship which Jesus advocates
and to which the disciples of a suffering Messiah should
be committed. This latter factor is seen clearly in 9:33–35;
10:23–31, 35–45. In 9:33–35, after Jesus for the second
time defines his messiahship in the nature of a suffering Son
of man (9:31), the disciples become involved in a discussion of their own merits. Jesus intervenes and admonishes
them against contemplation of personal grandeur and stipu-
lates that discipleship means a commitment to servanthood.
Likewise, in 10:35–45, following Jesus' third statement on
his christological position, James and John become involved
in a similar interest in prestige and honor. Once again Jesus
underscores the fact that discipleship cannot be measured
in terms of power or authority (10:42) but in terms of one's
dedication to being the servant of all (10:43–44). Similarly, in 10:23–31 one detects again the disciples' greater
concern for personal welfare and reward (10:23–28) than
for the kind of total self-sacrifice which characterizes authentic discipleship (8:34–35) and which Jesus demands of his
followers (10:21–22).[30]

This basic inability of the disciples to grasp or accept
Jesus' concept of messiahship or its corollary, suffering discipleship, becomes reflected more and more in their total
relationship to Jesus. The conflict over the correct inter-

30. I am dependent on Tyson, "Disciples," p. 264, for many of these
insights.

pretation of messiahship widens into a general conflict and misunderstanding in almost every area of their relationship with each other.

To illustrate: as Jesus' disciples, the disciples on one occasion are called upon to exorcise an unclean spirit, but they prove themselves incapable (9:15–18). When Jesus arrives on the scene, he despairs over this incapacity of his disciples (9:19–23) and quickly performs the requested exorcism (9:20–27). Since the Twelve still are not in harmony with Jesus and his mission, they are excoriated as a faithless group, as much without faith now as they were on the storm-tossed sea (4:40) and as unresponsive as the people in Jesus' home town (6:4 ff.).

On one occasion John and the others forbid a man to cast out demons (9:38), which causes Jesus to criticize them for their narrowness and interference (9:39–40). In another episode the disciples refuse to permit children to be brought to Jesus. In response to this rejection of the children Jesus becomes indignant, rebukes the disciples, and bids the children to come to him (10:13–16). Finally, by inserting 14:3–9 between 14:1–2 and 14:10 Mark leads the reader to believe that it was Judas' inability to understand Jesus' commendation of the woman's act of anointing that caused him to betray Jesus.[31]

The peculiarly Markan character and intensity of this theme is profoundly dramatized when one discovers the way in which Matthew and Luke react to this particular Markan motif. For the most part Matthew follows his usual practice of deleting or toning down unfavorable Markan comments about the disciples. He totally deletes the uncomplimentary Markan depiction of the disciples in Mark 9:5–6, 10, 32, 38–41. In Mark's narration of the scene in 9:33–37 he obviously focuses on the egocentric interests of the disciples in personal greatness. In Matthew (18:1–5) the disciples are no longer preoccupied with self-aggrandizement but instead ask what now appears to be an honest

31. See Schweizer, *The Good News*, p. 290.

and straightforward question about the characteristics of
greatness in the kingdom. While Matthew records the conflict between Jesus and the disciples over permitting children to come to him (19:13–15), he does tone down significantly Jesus' angry rebuke by removing the crucial comment
"he was indignant" from his text (19:14). Matthew has also
markedly altered the Markan account of James's and John's
bid for the key positions of honor in the new kingdom
(Mark 10:35 ff.). In the Matthean version the two brothers
have been cleared of any such personal greed, for it is not
they but their mother who presses Jesus in their behalf. One
can excuse a mother's importuning (20:20 ff.).

There are instances in which Matthew appears to preserve, contrary to his usual procedure, the degrading remarks or scenes from Mark. He certainly retains all the
bristling antipathy between Jesus and Peter found in Mark
8:32–33 (Matt. 16:22 ff.). Yet this sharp interchange, particularly Jesus' angry rebuke, has lost its Markan sharp edge
because of the previous Matthean investiture of Peter
(Matt. 16:17), an investiture absent in Mark. The discord,
noted by Mark in 10:23–31, between the disciples and Jesus
is also retained by Matthew. But here again the dissonance
has been partly softened by Matthew's addition of Jesus'
promise that the disciples will, because of their faithfulness
to him (Matt. 19:28), "sit on twelve thrones, judging the
twelve tribes of Israel" in the new kingdom. On the other
hand, Matthew preserves the full intensity of the clash between Jesus and the disciples in Mark 9:17 ff. (Matt. 17:
15 ff.) and portrays the disciples as the same disgruntled
people found in Mark 14:4 (Matt. 26:8). Despite these
exceptions Matthew basically follows the same procedure in
this Markan period as he did in the previous one. He consciously rewords the Markan material to enhance the presentation of the disciples.

When one turns to Luke and his treatment of the disciples in the Markan material in question, one is tempted to
conclude that Luke, unlike Matthew, concurs fully with
Mark in his poor rating of the disciples' performance with

their master. But such a conclusion would be drawn too hastily. For while it is true that Luke underscores the disciples' inability to comprehend the passion predictions, he adds a twist to the Markan presentation which really acquits the disciples from any responsibility for their obtuseness. It is God's plan that they should fail to understand the meaning or purpose of the passion (Luke 9:45). God purposely conceals from them all understanding of the suffering and death of Jesus until after the resurrection. Thus while Luke follows Mark in accenting the disciples' failure to comprehend the passion predictions (Luke 9:45; 18:34), Luke exculpates the disciples from the Markan insinuation that the cause of their failure to understand Jesus must be traced to them.[32]

There are also other indications that the third evangelist is interested in enhancing the image of the disciples. He omits the Markan reference to the disciples' obtuseness in Mark 9:10 (Luke 9:36). Much like Matthew, Luke softens the angry retort of Jesus to the disciples in Mark 10:14 by omitting "he was indignant" from his material (Luke 18:16). Some of the tarnish is also taken off the disciples in the Lucan version of Mark 10:23–31. In Luke's account (18: 24–30) the sermonic injunction about the handicap of riches is not directed to the disciples. Moreover, it is not explicitly the disciples who reply incredulously to Jesus' radical position. Peter does chime in at the end but only to attest to the faithfulness of the disciples, a faithfulness apparently acknowledged by Jesus (18:29–30).

On three occasions it would appear that Luke, however, is intent on collaborating with Mark in the denigration of the disciples. He makes no effort to change the poor performance of the disciples in Mark 9:33 ff. (Luke 9:46 ff.) and 9:38 ff. (Luke 9:49–50), and he introduces special material which culminates in a stinging rebuke of James and John (9:51–55). On the other hand, he certainly enhances the

32. See Conzelmann, *Luke*, pp. 56 ff., 64, 93, 151 ff., and Charles Talbert, *Luke and the Gnostics* (Nashville, Tenn.: Abingdon Press, 1966), pp. 40–41 on Luke's treatment of the Markan misunderstanding motif.

veneration of the disciples by his insertion of material con-
taining special blessings pronounced upon them (10:23–24)
and by Jesus' strong vindication of the disciples in the face
of the censuring effort of the Pharisees (Luke 19:39–40).
On the whole, despite the few exceptions in which Luke
plays into Mark's hand, the third evangelist follows essentially the same procedure as Matthew in redressing the
Markan maligning of the disciples.

Stage III: Rejection

With Judas' decision to betray Jesus to the religious hierarchy (14:10 ff.), Mark introduces the final phase in the
relationship between Jesus and his disciples. From 8:27 to
14:10 the conflict and tension between them were primarily
over a misconception of what constituted authentic messiahship. With Judas' plans to betray Jesus the conflict erupts
into an outright rejection of Jesus and his messiahship. That
this is true of all of the disciples and not just the traditional
villain, Judas, is substantiated by the episode in Gethsemane
and the incident in the courtyard of the high priest.

Despite the fact that the disciples assure Jesus of their
complete support of him in 14:31, they become indifferent
and unconcerned about him when put to the test. At one of
the most critical points in Jesus' life, when he ponders in the
garden over the fate that awaits him and to which he has
committed himself, Peter, James, and John remain completely oblivious of and apathetic toward the distress and
apprehension which has seized Jesus (14:32–42). Throughout this period of agonizing introspection Jesus implores his
special confidants to support him by watching and praying,
but on each of three separate occasions, after admonishing
them to remain awake, Jesus finds that they have fallen
asleep.

Subsequently, Jesus is betrayed by Judas (14:43–52) and
forsaken and abandoned by the rest (14:50). But it is the
denial of Peter that underscores the complete and utter rejection of Jesus and his messiahship by the disciples. Upon

the condemnation of the Sanhedrin, Peter completely renounces Jesus, adamantly denying that he ever knew him (14:66–72). The type of messiahship to which Jesus committed himself has now been totally rejected by the disciples.

How do Matthew and Luke treat the Markan picture at this point? Unlike the earlier stages of Mark's presentation, Matthew does not so obviously alter the Markan picture in this period of rejection. He follows his Markan source very closely in describing Judas' decision to betray (26:14–16), the scenes in Gethsemane (Matt. 26:36–46, 47–56), and the denial of Peter (26:66-75). The impact is the same as in Mark, and the disciples certainly fare no better.

The disciples experience far better treatment at Luke's hands. Just as their inability to understand Jesus' passion predictions was laid to the intention of God, so Judas' betrayal and Peter's denial are due to the work of Satan (22:3, 31). Peter and Judas are not really responsible for their rejection of Jesus. Unlike Mark and Matthew, Luke also attempts to remove the charge that the disciples lacked empathy with Jesus as he agonizes over his impending martyrdom. In the Lucan narrative the three occasions on which Jesus finds the disciples sleeping have been reduced to one, and in that case sleep comes upon them not because they are unconcerned about Jesus' fate. Quite the reverse, it is the emotional stress produced by their empathy that psychologically triggers sleep (22:40–45). Luke also rewrites the record to exonerate the disciples from the Markan indictment that they abandoned Jesus when the crowd came to apprehend him. Furthermore, the third evangelist has inserted in his narrative of the Last Supper a passage which clearly indicates that the disciples, far from rejecting or abandoning Jesus, are singled out by him as those who have been and will continue to be the most faithful (22:28 ff.).[33] In Luke's mind any unfavorable attitude or action by the disciples which may have occurred

33. Conzelmann, *Luke*, pp. 80 ff.

during the stress of the passion period cannot really be laid at their feet. Such out-of-character behavior is due to the work of Satan, whose seduction of them lies in the foreknowledge and plan of God. With the exception of Judas' and Peter's momentary lapse the disciples are models of true discipleship.

Conceding the fact that Matthew and Luke consciously alter the Markan denigration of the disciples, one might still want to ask whether this Markan motif really originates with or is actually peculiar to Mark. There is much about the fourth evangelist's depiction of the disciples' relationship with Jesus that reminds one of Mark. He emphasizes their lack of understanding of Jesus' teaching and activity more in the manner of Mark than does Matthew or Luke. But there are significant differences between the Markan and Johannine accounts. In John the disciples' lack of understanding never encompasses failure to recognize Jesus' messianic identity. From the beginning they acknowledge his christological nature (1:35–51). Moreover, Peter's confession and the title used by Peter in his confession indicates an extremely high degree of perception about the nature of the christological character which the Johannine Jesus claims for himself (6:68–69).[34] Unlike the Markan Twelve, the Johannine Twelve are not guilty of lack of faith or disbelief (2:11; 6:66 ff.; 16:30; 17:8). Nor can they ever be accused of obduracy. In John obduracy and disbelief are traits of the Jews (12:37–40).

John does preserve the tradition that Peter denied Jesus, Judas betrayed him, and the disciples abandoned him (18: 2 ff., 15–27; 16:32). But like Luke, John at least removes some of the onus of Judas' act from him by attributing it to the intervention of Satan (6:70–71). And the allusion to the disciples' abandonment of Jesus (16:32) implies that the disciples did not separate from Jesus solely of their own volition.

There is also a radical difference between John and Mark in the reference to the character of the disciples' lack of understanding and its duration. In John it is clear that the disciples do not always understand the meaning or import of Jesus' actions and teaching (11:7–16; 12:16; 13:6 ff.; 14: 4–9; 16:16 ff.). It is not clear, however, that they are intended to understand everything before Jesus' glorification (16:12–13, 25). After Jesus' glorification there is no doubt that the disciples are to be in a totally harmonious and fully cognitive relationship with Jesus. Any blindness or lack of understanding is completely dispelled with the resurrection (2:22; 12:16; 13:7). To make sure that such will be the case, the paraclete is sent to them (14:16–17; 16:7) to prod their memories and instruct in all matters (14:25–26; 16: 13). With the glorification the disciples are one with Jesus and the Father (17:6–26), a resolution in the disciples' relationship with Jesus significantly absent in Mark. To this we shall give attention shortly.

Our comparison of John with Mark, along with our analysis of the Matthean and Lucan response to Mark's presentation of the disciples, strongly indicates that we cannot attribute the dissonant relationship between Jesus and the disciples solely to the fanciful imagination of Mark.

But if not all the unfavorable presentation of the disciples can be traced to Mark, can the thoroughgoing programmatic denigration of the disciples be attributed to a Markan bias? I believe it can. While the tradition before Mark may have cited periods when Jesus' closest associates turned their backs on him, nowhere is there evidence that they were so completely recalcitrant as Mark would have us believe.

Paul certainly paints no such picture. It is an extremely curious phenomenon that Paul, with the exception of the betrayal (1 Cor. 11:23), never refers to the pre-Easter apostasy of the disciples. An argument from silence is never

conclusive. Yet such information about the disciples' dissonant relationship with and rejection of Jesus would have
been formidable ammunition for Paul at Antioch (Gal. 2:
11 ff.) and elsewhere in his contention that his own apostolic
credentials and kerygma were no less authentic or com-
mendatory than those of Peter and others who had been
with Jesus during his public ministry. If the disciples' response to Jesus was anywhere nearly as poor as Mark paints
it, it is hard to understand how Paul could have restrained
himself from drawing upon it for appropriate polemical or
apologetic purposes.

Several early non-Markan traditions, in fact, challenge the
almost totally negative profile of the disciples that Mark has
sketched. The few Q passages which address themselves to
the question of the disciples' relation to Jesus are all quite
positive and single out the disciples as a special group,
accorded singular honor and glory (Matt. 5:1 ff. ‖ Luke 6:
20 ff.; Matt. 13:16–17 ‖ Luke 10:23–24; Matt. 19:28 ‖ Luke
22:30). Of course, in light of Matthew's and Luke's correction of Mark's unfavorable picture of the disciples, it may
not have been in their interests to reproduce negative reflec-
tions on the disciples—though Luke apparently had no
qualms about introducing a non-Markan story concerning
an occasion when Jesus rebuked James and John (9:51–56).
But the point here is not whether or not Q contained uncomplimentary notes about the disciples. The point is that
Q did contain very positive comments on the disciples,
comments which place the disciples in a far more venerated
position than the evaluation they receive at the hands of
Mark. Nowhere in Mark are the disciples accorded such
approbation as: "Blessed are the eyes which see what you
see! For I tell you that many prophets and kings desired
to see what you see, and did not see it, and to hear what
you hear, and did not hear it" (Luke 10:23–24 ‖ Matt. 13:
16–17).

In Mark they have eyes but they never really see. They
have ears but never really hear (8:18). They are given the
mystery of the kingdom (4:11) but they never understand

(4:13; 7:18; 8:17, 21; 9:32). The Q passage places the disciples in the envious position of *seeing* what others have longed to see but did not. There is no suggestion that the disciples lack anything in visual and conceptual perception. Further, nowhere in Mark are the disciples promised seats of honor and power in the new kingdom as they are in Q, where they are promised elevation to the exalted position of judges "to sit on thrones judging the twelve tribes of Israel" (Luke 22:30 || Matt. 19:28).

Two sections of special Matthean and special Lucan material also challenge Mark's report: Matthew 16:17 ff. and Luke 22:31–32. The consensus among scholars is that behind Matthew 16:17 ff. lies an extremely old tradition.[35] Its apparent pre-Markan age offers convincing support for an early pre-Markan idealization of Peter, a process continued in Matthew and Luke but not perpetuated by Mark. Nowhere in Mark is Peter elevated to such a position of honor as he enjoys in this old Matthean tradition.

Likewise, the early age of Luke 22:31–32 is widely acclaimed.[36] Its importance for us is that it introduces us to a pre-Markan tradition which, against the Markan presentation of Peter's denial, suggests that Peter alone among the disciples did not turn against his Lord.[37] This in itself does not invalidate a claim that the Markan view, shared also by Matthew, Luke, and John, goes back to an authentic early tradition. But it does raise some doubt as to how much

35. See Bultmann, *History*, p. 259; A. Oepke, "Der Herrnspruch über die Kirche Matth. 16:17–19 in der neuesten Forschung," *ST* 2 (1950): 110 ff.; Oscar Cullmann, *Peter*, trans. F. V. Filson (Philadelphia: Westminster Press, 1953), p. 31; Bornkamm in Bornkamm, Barth, Held, *Tradition*, p. 45; Georg Strecker, *Der Weg der Gerechtigkeit* (Göttingen: Vandenhoeck & Ruprecht, 1966), p. 202.

36. See Bultmann, *History*, p. 267; Günter Klein, "Die Verleugnung des Petrus," *ZTK* 58 (1961): 302 ff.; Erich Dinkler, "Petrus-bekenntnis und Satanswort (Das Problem der Messianität Jesu)," *Zeit und Geschichte* (Bultmann festschrift), ed. Erich Dinkler (Tübingen: J. C. B. Mohr, 1964), p. 132.

37. Luke added v. 32b to this older tradition of vv. 31–32a in order to bring the non-Markan tradition and the tradition of Peter's denial—which he records subsequently (22:33–34, 54 ff.)—into some semblance of harmony. Cf. Bultmann, *History*, p. 267, and Klein, "Petrus," pp. 298 ff.

confidence can be placed in the historicity of the Markan position and certainly shows beyond question that there was no
uniform tradition about Peter's conduct in the last hours of
Jesus' life.

The non-Markan material we have looked at establishes
one important point. Some traditions prior to Mark had a
much higher regard for Peter and the disciples than Mark
chose to express. In contrast to the favorable presentations
of the disciples in these early non-Markan traditions, Mark
prefers to tell us the worst about the disciples.

The crowning evidence for attributing the programmatic,
denigrated picture of the disciples in Mark to the evangelist
himself lies in his treatment of, or rather his failure to treat,
the disciples after the denial of Peter. Following Peter's
denial the disciples do not reappear again in the narrative.
They cannot be found at the cross (15:22–41). They do not
share in the burial (15:42–47). They are not present at the
empty tomb (16:1–8). Yet the tradition of the early church
was that the witnesses of these kerygmatic events were the
disciples. By the time of Luke this was certainly an accepted
fact with regard to both the events of Jesus' earthly life and
the resurrection (Acts 1:21; 2:32; 3:15; 5:32; 10:39, 41). A
cardinal attestation of the budding Christian faith, according to the creed of 1 Corinthians 15:3–5, was that the
Twelve had witnessed the resurrection. Mark's successors
certainly shared this position (Matt. 28:16 ff.; Luke 24:34 ff.;
John 20:19 ff.). In Mark, however, the women alone are
witnesses to the death, burial, and most important of all,
the resurrection. What is even more startling, following
their total renunciation of Jesus, not only are the disciples
conspicuously absent from all subsequent events—even the
kerygmatic event upon which any claim for apostleship
must be based: the resurrection—but there is no indication
by Mark that the disciples were rehabilitated, that apostolicity *was* conferred upon them after their apostasy, as the
other evangelists clearly record (Matt. 28:16–20; Luke 24:
36–49; Acts 1:8; John 20:19–23).

I take such a position with regard to Mark convinced by the evidence that Mark intentionally ended his Gospel at 16:8, and thereby intended his reader to take the full implications of 16:8b seriously. How does the evidence support such an interpretation?

The debate over the abrupt ending of Mark has continued for a long time. A number of scholars have argued for linguistic and theological reasons that either there once was a longer conclusion which is now lost or Mark was providentially hindered from completing his work. The linguistic objections to 16:8 as the original conclusion of Mark have in my judgment been satisfactorily answered[38] and will not be rehearsed here.

Those who from a theological perspective find 16:8 to be an intolerable conclusion to a Gospel argue their case on the grounds that (1) it is psychologically offensive to the faith for the document to end on such a negative note[39] and (2) resurrection appearances must have been intended or certainly understood to have followed 16:8 because the early creeds refer to them, Mark 14:28 and 16:7 allude to them, and the other Gospels narrate them.[40] I find none of these arguments against the theological legitimacy of the abrupt Markan ending convincing.

The contention that the evangelist must have continued, or at least intended to continue, his narration beyond 16:8 with the traditional appearance narratives because the early creeds refer to them suffers from an ungrounded generalization. While it is true that one of the earliest creeds does

38. Cf. R. H. Lightfoot, *Locality and Doctrine in the Gospels* (London: Hodder & Stoughton, 1938), pp. 9–19, and idem, *The Gospel Message of Mark* (Oxford: Clarendon Press, 1950), pp. 86 ff.

39. W. L. Knox, "The Ending of St. Mark's Gospel," *HTR* 35 (1942): 22.

40. See, e.g., J. Finegan, *Die Überlieferung der Leidens–und Auferstehungsgeschichte Jesu* (Giessen: Alfred Töpelmann, 1934), p. 107; C. S. C. Williams, *Alterations to the Text of the Synoptic Gospels and Acts* (Oxford: Alden Press, 1961), pp. 43–44; C. E. B. Cranfield, *The Gospel According to Saint Mark* (Cambridge: Cambridge University Press, 1953), p. 471; Bultmann, *History*, pp. 285–86.

pointedly refer to such appearances (1 Cor. 15:5), a number of creedal statements do not refer to them at all (Rom. 1: 3–4; Phil. 2:6–11; 1 Tim. 3:16; 1 Pet. 3:18 ff.). The claim that 14:28 and 16:7 specifically allude to the appearances, and thus confirm the evangelist's intent to narrate them following the empty-grave story, has been formidably challenged by a number of Markan scholars who contend persuasively that 14:28 and 16:7 do not allude to the resurrection appearances at all but point to the impending parousia.[41]

The assertion that the presence of resurrection appearances in the other Gospels justifies viewing Mark as incomplete without them smacks of the logical fallacy of the conclusion dictating the premise. To argue that Mark must have followed the same procedure as other Christian writers who wrote similar compositions violates the integrity of Mark by forcing it to harmonize with its literary descendants. Such a procedure totally obliterates the unique literary particularities of the Markan composition and denies the evangelist the possibility of being guided by his own peculiar interests, some of which may have placed him out of step with the rest of the Christian movement. Aside from this, it strikes me as methodologically unsound to base an argument on the one-time existence of material for which absolutely no extant trace has been found. One sometimes wonders if the proponents of a "lost conclusion" are not more interested in harmonizing the literary and theological characteristics of early Christian literature than with defending the integrity and particularity of the Markan composition.

Methodologically it is far sounder to seek the answer to the peculiarities of a composition from internal evidence of the extant text rather than from external factors, real or

41. See Ernst Lohmeyer, *Galiläa und Jerusalem* (Göttingen: Vandenhoeck and Ruprecht, 1936), and idem, *Das Evangelium des Markus*, 15th ed. (Göttingen: Vandenhoeck and Ruprecht, 1959), p. 356; Lightfoot, *Locality*, pp. 63 ff., 73 ff.; Willi Marxsen, *Mark the Evangelist*, trans. R. A. Harrisville et al. (Nashville, Tenn.: Abingdon Press, 1969), pp. 75 ff.; Neill Q. Hamilton, "Resurrection Tradition and the Composition of Mark," *JBL* 84 (1965): 421; Norman Perrin, "Towards an Interpretation of the Gospel of Mark," an unpublished paper.

envisioned. If what has struck Mark's contemporaries (Matthew and Luke) and subsequent readers of the Gospel as theologically intolerable can be adequately explained from internal evidence, then there is no need to risk violating the integrity of the composition by hypothesizing upon what the "original" state of the composition might have been.

I believe internal evidence provides us with an appropriate and adequate explanation for the Gospel's terminating at 16:8. Ludger Schenke has recently carried out a provocative and in my judgment persuasive redaction-critical investigation of the empty-tomb story. His results have unearthed a pre-Markan narrative consisting of 16:2, 5, 6, 8a. Mark took this source, added his own remarks at 16:1, 3–4, 7, 8b, and with the resulting composition closed his Gospel.[42]

Schenke builds his argument for the Markan appending of 16:8b to the conclusion (16:8a) of an empty-tomb story on the contention that 16:7 is a Markan insertion into that story, a position a number of scholars hold.[43] If 16:7 is a Markan addition, Schenke argues, the climactic and emphatic point of the original story must have been the message of the angel in 16:6. In the original story, then, the description of the women's experience of numinous awe (16:8a) serves as a natural conclusion. But not so for 16:8b. Its presence at the conclusion of a narrative which did not originally contain 16:7 creates an awkward tension in the account. The repeated emphasis upon the response of the women to the event tends to distract attention from the primary point of the story (16:6) and draw it to a secondary feature, the enigmatic reaction of the women. Moreover,

---

42. Ludger Schenke, *Auferstehungsverkündigung und leeres Grab*, Stuttgarter Bibelstudien, no. 33 (Stuttgart: Katholisches Bibelwerk, 1969), pp. 30–55.

43. See Bultmann, *History*, p. 285; Martin Dibelius, *From Tradition to Gospel*, trans. B. L. Woolf (New York: Charles Scribner's Sons, 1935), p. 190; Erich Klostermann, *Das Markusevangelium*, Handbuch zum Neuen Testament, no. 3 (Tübingen: J. C. B. Mohr [Paul Siebeck], 1950), p. 171; Marxsen, *Mark*, pp. 75 ff.; Schreiber, "Die Christologie," p. 176; Hans Grass, *Ostergeschehen und Osterberichte*, 3d ed. (Göttingen: Vandenhoeck and Ruprecht, 1964), p. 21.

Schenke argues, the way in which the fear response is reported in 16:8b with the statement, "they said nothing to any one for they were afraid" introduces an apologetic thrust to the narrative unwarranted up to that point.

Not only does the presence of 16:8b produce ambiguity as to where the focal point of the story lies, but it also introduces a conceptual dissonance. Schenke points out that the description of psychological response in 16:8a is clearly that of numinous awe, a positive expression of fear. The fear referred to in 16:8b, however, is negative, cowardly fear.

Schenke posits that the best explanation for 16:8b is that it was added by the evangelist as a sequel to his comment in 16:7. So viewed, 16:8b reports the way in which the women responded to the command of the angel.[44] This line of argument makes sense. For it is the insertion of 16:7 into the empty-tomb story that shifts the emphasis to the women and their response and alters their function in the drama. Without 16:7 the women serve only as spectators to the supernatural event. What the women did subsequent to the encounter with the angel in 16:6 is not central to the point of the story. With the addition of 16:7 they become active agents in the resurrection with responsibility to communicate the angel's message. Consequently, a word is needed about the way in which the women executed the angel's command. The original reference to their running away in awe is inadequate for this purpose. Mark 16:8b was required to indicate that the command of the angel failed to be executed because the fear which the women experienced incapacitated them.

Additional corroborative evidence for Schenke's position on 16:8a and b is appropriately noted here. Linguistically the fact that ἔκστασις (astonishment, ecstasy) is found only one other time in Mark (and that, 5:42, in his received material) and the fact that the occurrence of τρόμος (trembling) in 16:8a is its only occurrence in the New Testament support a non-Markan identification of 16:8a. On the other

44. Schenke, *Grab*, pp. 47 ff.

hand, the Markan stylistic use of οὐδείς (no one) in combination with another negative requiring the indicative mood[45] and his proclivity for φοβεῖσθαι (to fear) in the third person plural, imperfect tense, passive voice[46] argue in favor of the Markan creation of 16:8b.

Even more significant is the presence in 16:8 of the Markan practice of intentionally creating abrupt and unexpected shifts in psychological emphasis and direction of thought by appending editorial comments to received material. Cases elsewhere in Mark which immediately come to mind are those in which the evangelist has affixed commands of silence to messianic confessions and miraculous acts of Jesus where one might normally expect their proclamation to be encouraged (e.g., 5:42–43; 7:35–36; 8:27–30; 9:9). More to the present point are those places where in the course of editing the evangelist has linked responses of cowardly fear to experiences of the numinous (4:41; 9:5–6) and juxtaposed responses of awe and cowardly fear (10:32; 11:18).[47] In this respect the passage that comes closest to paralleling the circumstances and linguistic character of 16:8 is 6:51–52. The point of the original conclusion to the pre-Markan story of Jesus walking on water (6:51) was to underscore the ecstatic response of awe to what in all likelihood was originally a post-Easter appearance story.[48] The verb ἐξίστασθαι (to be amazed) is used here just as it and the noun ἔκστασις were used in 5:42 and as the noun alone was

---

45. This stylistic use of οὐδείς is more characteristic of Mark (3:27; 5:3, 37; 6:5; 7:12; 9:8; 11:2; 12:14, 34; 14:60, 61; 15:4, 5; 16:8) than any other New Testament author except John. Matthew renders the Markan usage only at Matt. 22:16 (Mark 12:14); Luke, only at Luke 20:40 (Mark 12:34), despite the fact that he evidences a proclivity for this stylistic trait in passages where Mark does not use it.

46. This particular form of the verb occurs five times in Mark (9:32; 10:32; 11:18, 32; 16:8), only six times in the New Testament outside of Mark. Mark 9:32; 10:32; and 11:18 are clearly redactional uses of the word.

47. Cf. Lyder Brun, *Die Auferstehung Christi in der urchristlichen Ueberlieferung* (Oslo: H. Aschehoug & Co. [W. Nygaard], 1925), p. 9; Schenke, *Grab*, p. 49; cf. Schweizer, *The Good News*, pp. 216–17, on 10:32 and 11:18.

48. Bultmann, *History*, p. 230.

used in 16:8, namely, to depict the psychological reaction
of awe. Beyond doubt the original psychological tone of
the conclusion (6:51) to the epiphany of the Lord prior to
Mark's use was thoroughly positive.[49] Mark's appending of
6:52 to this story has changed an original hospitable, ecstatic response to Jesus into a psychologically negative reaction. The disciples not only do not receive Jesus with
reverence but they are obdurate.

Mark intentionally affixed 16:8b to 16:8a as his final editorial comment in his work. The effect, of course, is a
startling, and to many an offensive, suggestion that the
disciples never received the angel's message, thus never met
the resurrected Lord, and, consequently never were commissioned with apostolic rank after their apostasy. As inconceivable as this suggestion may be at first blush, it is in
complete harmony with Mark's attitude toward and treatment of the disciples throughout his Gospel. Mark 16:8b
must be read at full face value with all its sundry ramifications![50]

I conclude that Mark is assiduously involved in a vendetta against the disciples. He is intent on totally discredit-
ing them. He paints them as obtuse, obdurate, recalcitrant

---

49. This is certainly Matthew's interpretation of the experience (14:33).
John's account of the story also stresses a positive emotion in the disciples'
reception of Jesus once he identifies himself (6:20–21).

50. Only recently has the thought occurred that 16:8b could have
apologetic implications with regard to a particular theological perspective
in the church. Schreiber, "Die Christologie," pp. 178–79 and Schenke,
Grab, p. 51, interpret Mark 16:8 as an explanation for why it was that
the church at Jerusalem did not respond to the Hellenistic mission,
symbolized geographically by Galilee. In his book Theologie, pp. 13–14,
Schreiber speaks more in terms of a polemic against Peter and the
Twelve. Cf. also Trocmé, La Formation, pp. 100 ff. Most scholars have
failed to recognize the full ramifications of 16:8b as a polemic against the
Twelve either because they have interpreted the passage as part of the
messianic secret (Marxsen, Mark, p. 91) or because they could not con-
ceive of anyone in the early church defaming the disciples (e.g., Meye,
Jesus, p. 85; Quesnell, Mark, p. 170). Klein, "Petrus," pp. 312 ff., believes
it is not inconceivable that factions in the early church could have
engaged in a character assassination of Peter as a result of the power
plays that went on in the church. He believes that the story of Peter's
denial of Jesus may have been the legendary creation of those opposed
to Peter.

men who at first are unperceptive of Jesus' messiahship, then oppose its style and character, and finally totally reject it. As the coup de grace, Mark closes his Gospel without rehabilitating the disciples.

Positing such a radical turn in the interpretation and understanding of Mark's treatment of the Twelve obviously raises a bevy of questions that must be satisfactorily answered if this position is to be convincing. Primary among such questions is the query as to why Mark would deviate so radically from the trend in the rest of Christian literature and wage this devastating attack on the Twelve. It is to this question that the discussion now turns.

II

The Christological Conflict

The source of conflict between the Markan disciples and the Markan Jesus is clearly christological. While the disciples' christological disagreement with Jesus remains primarily subliminal prior to the Petrine confession, with the dialogue at Caesarea Philippi it emerges sharply, arrives quickly at full intensity, and culminates in the disciples' rejection of Jesus' messiahship. There can be little doubt that christology is the issue that divides Jesus and his confidants. From the explosive exchange between Peter and Jesus to the betrayal, abandonment, and denial, the question of authentic messiahship (8:29–33; 9:30–32; 10:32–34, 45) or its corollary, authentic discipleship (8:34–38; 9:33–37; 10:35–44), remains the primary source of dissonance. It follows logically that an identification and delineation of the conflicting christological points of view can provide important clues to the purpose of Mark's vendetta against the disciples.

The Markan Jesus' Christology

There is no particular problem in identifying Jesus' christological position. Authentic messiahship is suffering messiahship which leads inevitably to crucifixion. No reader of Mark could mistake this. The evangelist underscores the suffering-servant role of Jesus in the passion predictions and other allusions Jesus makes to his suffering and death (8:31; 10:38–39, 45; 12:7–8; 14:8, 24, 27, 34 ff.). Second, Mark accentuates the suffering role of Jesus through the motif of the disciples' misconception of messiahship. By dramatizing the misunderstanding of the disciples and their ensuing conflict with Jesus over his concept of the suffering

Son of man, the evangelist emblazons in bold relief the nature of Jesus' messiahship. Third, Mark reinforces the concept of suffering messiahship by devoting extensive attention to its corollary, suffering discipleship (8:34–35, 10:28–30, 43–44; 13:9–13). Fourth, he gives central importance to the recounting of the passion narrative.

Finally, Mark seeks to convince the reader that Jesus' role as a suffering servant was not only the central and most important element in his messiahship but was the role specifically ordained by God and the role by which he was finally accurately identified by man. God's ordaining of the suffering Son-of-man role is accentuated most clearly in 9:7 and 14:36. Contrary to some opinions, the heavenly voice in 9:7 does not confirm the confession of Peter. Rather, it is the divine sanctioning of the suffering-servant role which Jesus has just proclaimed for himself and which Peter has rejected (8:31–32).[1] This is precisely the reason why the words ἀκούετε αὐτοῦ (hear him) follow the divine confirmation of sonship. They are to be understood as a command to Peter and the others to accept Jesus' definition of messiahship. Likewise, through the account of Jesus' acceptance of the cup of suffering willed by God (14:35–36), the evangelist dramatically demonstrates that the whole course of suffering and death which Jesus follows is as God has willed it.

The centurion's confession (15:39) underscores the fact that man can only perceive the nature of Jesus' messiahship (sonship) when he recognizes him as the suffering Son of man.[2] The crucial point in this unexpected proclamation of the centurion is that he recognized and confessed Jesus to be the Son of God solely upon witnessing Jesus' suffering

1. So Eduard Schweizer, *The Good News According to Mark*, trans. D. H. Madvig (Richmond, Va.: John Knox Press, 1970), p. 182; Johannes Schreiber, *Theologie des Vertrauens* (Hamburg: Furche-Verlag H. Rennebach K. G., 1967), pp. 120, 230; Neill Q. Hamilton, *Jesus for a No-God World* (Philadelphia: Westminster Press, 1969), p. 145.

2. Cf. Ulrich Luz, "Das Geheimnismotiv und die Markanische Christologie," ZNW 56 (1965): 26.

and death. That Jesus is the Son of God or Messiah entirely by virtue of his suffering path in life and death is a conclusion that Mark refuses to let his reader avoid.

The Disciples' Christology

Identifying the christological position of the Markan Jesus is accomplished with ease. Determining the christological position of the Markan disciples is far more difficult. The first indication of their messianic concept is found in the Caesarea Philippi episode, where Peter recognizes Jesus as the Messiah. Precisely what the Petrine concept of messiahship entails is not explicitly stated by the evangelist. Negatively, one can be certain that by Messiah Peter and the disciples did not have in mind suffering messiahship. Peter adamantly rejects such an idea (8:32).

One of the best clues to an understanding of the disciples' position lies in the first half of the Gospel, before 8:29. At first glance the material prior to 8:29 sheds no light on Peter's sudden revelation. Yet the inability to recognize the clues which point to the conceptual basis for such a revelation may be the fault of the modern reader. It is difficult to read Mark without bringing to it consciously or unconsciously an awareness of the other Gospels and the rest of the New Testament literature which, by virtue of our knowledge of this material, must color, if not in some cases distort, any reading or interpretation of Mark. One cannot assume that the first readers of Mark had the benefit of the full breadth of the Christian tradition which the non-Markan material of Matthew, Luke, and John offers contemporary scholarship. A more accurate interpretation, and one less subject to error, is arrived at when Mark is approached in the way the first reader approached it: without preconceived knowledge of its contents and without the prejudicial knowledge of the other Gospels.

If the Gospel is so read, when the reader arrives at the point of Peter's confession he has no recourse but to assume that whatever insights dawned upon Peter must have grown out of a recognition of the nature of Jesus revealed to the disciples (and to the reader) prior to the confession. What, then, is the picture of Jesus revealed to the reader?

In the past decade an increasing number of Markan scholars have recognized that a large amount of Markan material is steeped in a christology drawn in the tradition of the Hellenistic *theios aner* (divine man).[3] In such a perspective Jesus is characterized as the epiphany of God, the divine savior in human form, who intervenes in human affairs to work miracles in behalf of man. He is not a deity, but superhuman—a combination of the divine and human. He is embued with the power and authority of God, and possesses supernatural knowledge and wisdom which he selectively reveals as divine revelation to those of his own choosing.[4]

---

3. Helmut Koester, "Häretiker im Urchristentum," *RGG*[3] 3 (1959): 18–19, and idem, "One Jesus and Four Primitive Gospels," *HTR* 61 (1968): 230 ff.; Johannes Schreiber, "Die Christologie des Markusevangeliums," *ZTK* 58 (1961): 154–83, and idem, *Theologie;* James M. Robinson, "The Recent Debate on the 'New Quest,'" *JBR* 30 (1962): 203–4, and idem, "Kerygma and History in the New Testament," *The Bible in Modern Scholarship*, ed. J. P. Hyatt (Nashville, Tenn.: Abingdon Press, 1965), pp. 133 ff.; Philipp Vielhauer, "Erwägungen zur Christologie des Markusevangeliums," *Zeit und Geschichte* (Bultmann festschrift), ed. Erich Dinkler (Tübingen: J. C. B. Mohr, 1964), pp. 155–69; Luz, "Das Geheimnismotiv," pp. 9–30; Eduard Schweizer, "Zur Frage des Messiasgeheimnisses bei Markus," *ZNW* 56 (1965): 8; Leander Keck, "Mark 3.7–12 and Mark's Christology," *JBL* 84 (1965): 341–58; H. Dieter Betz, "Jesus as Divine Man," *Jesus and the Historian* (Colwell festschrift), ed. F. Thomas Trotter (Philadelphia: Westminster Press, 1965), pp. 114–33; Paul J. Achtemeier, "Toward the Isolation of Pre-Markan Miracle Catenae," *JBL* 89 (1970): 265–91; Norman Perrin, "The Christology of Mark: A Study in Methodology," (paper presented at the Seminar on Christology of the New Testament at the Annual Meeting of the Studiorum Novi Testamenti Societas, New Castle upon Tyne, England, August 1970).

4. Throughout this book the Hellenistic view of Jesus (and others) as "divine man" will be indicated through the use of the term *theios aner.* By using *theios aner* as a technical term for the "divine-man" phenomenon attention is focused more precisely on the Hellenistic religious phenomenon than through use of the English translation of the Greek term. The English translation ("divine man") is subject to too many ambiguous connotations suggested by various popular usages of the concept "divine man" in currency today. Where it is necessary in the course of the book to refer to more than one *theios aner,* the anglicized form of the Greek plural will be used, namely, *theioi andres* (divine men).

When one examines the Markan material prior to the Petrine confession, one is overwhelmed by the amount of material that is oriented to this particular christological perspective.[5] The heavy emphasis on the *theios-aner* motif in the material prior to the Petrine confession could not be lost on Mark's first readers. If the only portion of Mark's Gospel one possessed was 1:1–8:29, one would have to assume that Mark understood Jesus to be a *theios aner* and that his messiahship was to be interpreted only within this perspective. There is absolutely no hint in the first half of the Gospel that authentic messiahship should contain any other christological dimension. There is no trace of the suffering Son-of-man motif that dominates the last half of the Gospel (e.g., 8:31; 9:31; 10:33–34, 45; 14:24). It is true that there is an allusion to a plot against Jesus in 3:6, but there is absolutely no suggestion, even at this point, that Jesus' messianic role should follow the suffering servant's path of humiliation and death.[6] The dark omen of 3:6 serves quite appropriately as the forewarning of the death of the *theios aner* at the hands of his enemies.

But it is not just the fact that the evangelist has saturated his Gospel with the miracle-working picture of Jesus prior to 8:29 that convinces me that he intended the reader to draw the conclusion that Peter's confession is to be understood as a confession to a *theios-aner* Christ. Mark deftly employs two other literary techniques to force this conclusion upon the reader. One such technique we have already discussed rather completely in another connection. That is the way in which Mark underscores the radical differences between the disciples and the populace in their perception of and response to Jesus. The contrast is illustrated most fully and dramatically in the reactions to Jesus as a

5. Mark 1:9–13, 23–24, 40–45; 2:1–12; 3:1–12; 4:35–41; 5:1–43; 6:1–6, 34–56; 7:24–37; 8:1–10, 22–26. Cf. discussions on this material by Betz, "Jesus," pp. 117 ff.; Keck, "Mark's Christology," pp. 341 ff.; Erich Grässer, "Jesus in Nazareth (Mark VI. 1–6a)," *NTS* 16 (1969): 1–23; Achtemeier, "Miracle Catenae," pp. 265 ff.

6. Cf. Quentin Quesnell, *The Mind of Mark*, Analecta Biblica, no. 38 (Rome: Pontifical Biblical Institute, 1969); pp. 131–32, whose argument runs in the same vein.

miracle worker. The disciples, though constant companions of Jesus throughout his miracle-working activity, fail to perceive or respond to these powers of Jesus. Yet others far less intimately associated with Jesus recognize his special powers immediately and respond without hesitation to him as a *theios aner* (1:32–34; 2:1–12; 3:7–12; 5:1–43; 6:53–56; 7:24–37; 8:22–26), placing faith in him as such (2:5; 5:34, cf. 1:32, 40; 3:10; 5:22–23; 7:28–29, 32; 8:22). The evangelist's repeated staging of this ironic contrast in response to Jesus' miracle-working powers creates two effects on the mind of the reader. It concentrates attention on Jesus' role as a *theios aner*. It provokes the question: When are the disciples going to recognize that Jesus is a *theios aner*?[7]

The other technique Mark uses to persuade the reader that Peter proclaims a *theios-aner* christology is the employment of an identity motif.[8] The subject of Jesus' identity arises repeatedly in the course of the narrative from 1:1– 8:29. Human participants in the drama pose the question of identity on numerous occasions: the crowd after an exorcism (1:27), the scribes when Jesus heals the paralytic (2:5 ff.), the disciples after Jesus calms the tempestuous sea (4:41), Jesus' home town neighbors in response to Jesus' unusual wisdom and miraculous powers (6:2 ff.), Herod and his associates upon news of the supernatural powers of the Jesus circle (6:14–16). Demonic forces proclaim Jesus' identity when Jesus exorcises them (1:24, 34; 3:11; 5:7). God announces it at the baptism (1:11). Jesus announces it in the course of healing the paralytic (2:5 ff.) and in the dispute over picking grain on the sabbath (2:28). The evangelist proclaims it in the opening verse of his Gospel.

The striking fact about this identity motif is that it almost invariably emerges in the context of Jesus' miracle-working

7. Cf. Quesnell, *Mark*, pp. 161–70.

8. Quesnell, *Mark*, pp. 157–61, 170–71, also sees the importance of the identity motif as a technique employed by the evangelist to shape his reader's thinking.

activity. In fact, Jesus himself presses the identity question on the disciples immediately upon his restoration of
the blind man's sight (8:22–26). This repeated interest in
Jesus' identity resulting from his success as a *theios aner*
cannot have been lost on the mind of the Hellenistic reader.
The evangelist leaves him no option but to conclude that
there is an intrinsic relationship between Jesus' divinely
ordained office as Messiah and his activity as a *theios aner*,
a relationship which, after Jesus' prodding, finally dawned
upon Peter.[9]

Mark's schematic arrangement of his material in 1:1–
8:29, in which the presentation of Jesus as a *theios aner*
culminates in a christological confession to a *theios-aner*
Christ, is not unique. This Markan hermeneutical process
comes remarkably close to duplicating in content and structure the same pattern behind the Signs Source of John.

9. Koester, "Jesus," p. 232, argues that in the New Testament titles
such as "Christ" and "Son of God" are usually linked to *theios-aner*
christology. One might object to the argumentation up to this point
thusly: if Jesus' miracle-working activity places him in the role of a
theios aner, a role which the populace recognized, how is it that this
same populace identified him with such figures as John the Baptist, or
Elijah, or a prophet (6:15; 8:28)? To identify Jesus with these figures
by virtue of his *theios-aner* activity would not be unusual at all for a
Hellenistic audience (Jewish or Christian). While Elijah is normally
thought of as the eschatological prophet, the forerunner of the Messiah,
he was also looked upon in Hellenistic Judaism as a *theios aner* (cf. Dieter
Georgi, *Die Gegner des Paulus im 2. Korintherbrief* [Neukirchen-Vluyn:
Neukirchener Verlag, 1964], pp. 148, 216), one who intercedes for the
elect, healing the sick, and so on (cf. Joachim Jeremias, " ʾΗλ(ε)ίας,"
TDNT 2:930). It is precisely this picture of Elijah as a *theios aner* which
one finds in Mark 9:2–8 (so Georgi, *Die Gegner*, p. 216) and 15:35. It is
true that Mark pictures Elijah as the eschatological prophet (cf. 9:11–13);
but that does not negate the fact that some of Mark's sources pictured
Elijah as a *theios aner*. Similarly, the title of prophet would also be at
home in the *theios-aner* perspective, particularly when one thinks in terms
of the Mosaic-prophet typology, a typology that we find drawn upon, e.g.,
in the Signs Source of John (cf. J. Louis Martyn, *History and Theology
in the Fourth Gospel* [New York: Harper & Row, 1969], pp. 91 ff.;
Robert T. Fortna, *The Gospel of Signs* [Cambridge: Cambridge University
Press, 1970], p. 230), in Luke 24:19 and Acts 3:12–26; 7:35 ff. (cf.
Howard Teeple, *The Mosaic Eschatological Prophet* [Philadelphia: Society
of Biblical Literature, 1957], pp. 74–94; Joachim Jeremias, "Μωυσῆς"
TDNT 4:864–71; Georgi, *Die Gegner*, p. 216–17). The reference to John
the Baptist is to John redivivus, not the "historical" John. In the popular
mentality of the day it is easy to understand why one raised from the
dead would be looked upon as a *theios aner*.

A number of scholars have argued that the Signs Source consisted of a collection of Jesus' wonder-working activities, which concluded with the following christological affirmation: "Now Jesus did many other signs in the presence of the disciples, which are not written in this book; but these are written that you may believe that Jesus is the Christ, the Son of God" (John 20:30–31).[10] Helmut Koester and Robert Fortna have recently argued that this source emerged from a Christian community of a *theios-aner* orientation, which sought to present Jesus as a great *theios aner* whose miracles point to and demonstrate the fact that he is the Messiah.[11] The parallel to Mark 1:1–8:29 is obvious. The author (or authors) of the Signs Source persuaded his reader that Jesus was the Christ by narrating one sign after another until the reader was forced to conclude what the author intended him to conclude: the Jesus of the signs, the *theios aner* from Nazareth, is the Christ. Analogously, Mark narrates Jesus' miracles one after another *in the presence of his disciples* (so John 20:30), capping the narration with a confession to Jesus as a *theios-aner* Christ.

The *Theios-Aner* Discipleship of the Disciples

There is also abundant evidence after the Petrine confession that the evangelist pictured Peter and the disciples as acclaiming *theios-aner* christology. Most of this evidence lies in the type of discipleship which they choose for themselves. But this is a logical place to find christology implicitly stated. The way in which one formulates christology determines one's formulation of discipleship. Obviously the best evidence for this in Mark is the correspondence that the Markan Jesus himself points out between authentic christology and authentic discipleship (8:34 ff. vis-à-vis 8:31).

10. See Robinson, "Kerygma," pp. 136 ff. for bibliographical data and his insights on the relationship between the Signs Source, Mark, and other New Testament literature. Cf. also Koester, "Jesus," p. 232, and Fortna, *Signs*, pp. 197 ff.

11. Fortna, *Signs*, pp. 221–34; Koester, "Jesus," pp. 230 ff. Cf. also the important study by Fortna's teacher, J. Louis Martyn, *Fourth Gospel*, pp. 91 ff.

If there is such a close correspondence between suffering-servanthood christology and suffering-servanthood disciple-ship, one would then expect the same correspondence be-tween christology and discipleship to be found in *theios-aner* perspective. For the purpose of our discussion Dieter Georgi's significant work, focusing on Paul's last series of correspondence with Corinth, is extremely important. Georgi's study provides us with a profile of the *theios-aner* discipleship in Corinth against which to view the disciple-ship position of the Markan disciples, in our quest to deter-mine to what extent the Markan disciples reflect the *theios-aner* orientation in their discipleship. According to Georgi,[12] Paul's enemies in this particular correspondence (2 Cor. 2:14–7:4; 10–13) saw themselves as great miracle workers. In fact they believed that the power of Jesus as a divine man was now embodied and revealed in their own lives. This was possible because they blurred, if not completely obliterated, the distinction between the historical Jesus and the postresurrection exalted Lord. Ignoring the clear-cut break (the crucifixion) between the historical Jesus and the resurrected Lord, these opponents of Paul conceived of the power and pneumaticism of Jesus as continuing to mani-fest itself without break and without loss of continuity or efficacy in their own *theios-aner* activity. Consequently, the canonical measurement for the quality of Christian life for them was determined by the quantity, magnitude, and spectacular character of their miraculous acts and pneumatic experiences.

Such a mind-set permits no place for weakness, failure, or second place. The focus is on success against impossible odds and victory where others have failed. One must prove himself entitled to the veneration of his followers by being superior to others in supernatural power and spiritual ex-perience. It is not surprising, then, to find Paul's *theios-aner* opponents reveling in competition with each other,

---

12. What follows is a condensation of Georgi's argument (*Die Gegner*, pp. 219–305). Cf. also Robinson's discussion and elaboration on Georgi's position, "Kerygma," pp. 140 ff., and Koester, "Jesus," pp. 230 ff.

making extravagant claims for themselves in the face of the claims of others. With unabashed self-righteous pride they boasted of their pneumatic gifts, ecstatic experiences, and miraculous feats. They enjoyed most of all flaunting their superiority over others less spiritually mature. Doting upon their sense of superiority, they conceived of themselves as an elite group in the community. Because of their special pneumatic experiences, to which others less meritorious were not privileged, they claimed they were custodians of a secret gospel. Their preaching was allegorical and its meaning purposely concealed, since the secret of their hidden gospel had to be kept within their exclusive ranks.

The profile of the Corinthian *theioi andres* (divine men) serves as a suggestive model against which one can compare the discipleship attitudes of the Markan disciples. In this way one can gauge to what degree they reflect the *theios-aner* perspective. When such a comparison is made, striking correspondence emerges. In the first place, one should note the presentation of discipleship which lies behind Mark 3:15; 6:7, 13. On these particular occasions Jesus, acting in the capacity of a *theios aner*, bestows upon his disciples his own special authority to perform miraculous feats. The result is that they are successful miracle workers (6:13).[13] In the second place, the disciples, like the Corinthian heretics, appear to be the receivers and custodians of a secret gospel. At least from passages such as 4:10–12, 33–34; 7:17 ff.; 8:14–21, 30–31; 9:2–13, 30–32, 33 ff.; 10:10 ff., 32–34; 13:3 ff., one must surmise that the disciples are instructed in and are exposed to things which those outside their elite circle are not privileged to know or experience. And on the basis of 4:10–12, 33–34 it would appear that the nature of this instruction is more than just

---

13. The reader undoubtedly recognizes an inconsistency at this point. Earlier in our discussion it was suggested that the disciples were unperceptive of Jesus as a miracle worker. Yet now I am arguing that they have accepted the commission to be miracle workers and are successful. How can they fail to recognize Jesus, yet perform miracles themselves as Jesus' representatives? The answer to this apparent contradiction must be delayed for now but will be discussed later; see pp. 167–68.

that which might naturally be given to trusted companions
as distinct from the general populace. The disciples are,
in fact, described as custodians of an esoteric message whose
mystery is purposely to remain obscure to those on the outside (4:11–12). Its secret meaning is understood only
through allegorical interpretation (4:13 ff.).

Some of the most striking *theios-aner* traits of the disciples come into focus when they are seen over against the
suffering discipleship which Jesus advocates (8:34 ff.).
Illustrating these conflicting points of view are the passages
9:33–37 and 10:35–44. Like the heretics in 2 Corinthians,
the disciples in 9:33–37 are engaged in comparing themselves with each other to determine who is the greatest
among them. Jesus intervenes in the discussion and sharply
reprimands the disciples for placing such importance upon
rank, honor, and self-praise. He proclaims that the real
sign of greatness lies in servanthood to all (9:35). A similar
confrontation of Jesus with his disciples over the question
of merit and honor is found in 10:35–44. In this instance
James and John importune Jesus for the right to hold the
highest positions of honor in his glory (10:35–37). Jesus
rejects their request and in the ensuing discussion suggests
that the disciples have an entirely erroneous attitude toward
discipleship. Instead of acting like the leaders of the Gentiles, who enjoy ruling over and lording their authority over
their fellow men, his disciples must accept positions of total
humility and be servants to all (10:41–44).

In line with this, 9:38–41 deserves attention, for it points
to another area of similarity between the position of the
disciples in Mark and the heretics in Corinth. Long ago
Johannes Weiss claimed that 9:33–41 was a polemic against
the disciples.[14] The point of the scene appears to be an
attack upon the ambition of the disciples (9:33–37) and
their claims to exclusive authority (9:38–41). Clearly, one
finds here a dispute over the relation of the members of
the Christian community to each other. So viewed, v. 37

14. Johannes Weiss, *Das älteste Evangelium* (Göttingen: Vandenhoeck and
Ruprecht, 1903), pp. 257 ff.

speaks to the question of a person's qualifications to be a member of the community. Using a child as an example, the Markan Jesus illustrates that the most humble and insignificant person is worthy of acceptance and esteem in the community. To receive such a person is analogous to accepting Christ himself.

But the disciples are not so benevolent toward or receptive of other Christians, as 9:38–41 shows us. The crux of the problem in 9:38 is not that the exorcist is a non-Christian performing an exorcism in the name of Christ. Quite the contrary, the person in question is a Christian exorcist who is not part of the disciples' group.[15] The disciples' objections center around the words ὃς οὐκ ἀκολουθεῖ ἡμῖν (who does not follows us), and οὐκ ἠκολούθει ἡμῖν (he was not following us). The issue is not whether he follows Jesus. He obviously follows Jesus because his exorcism is done under Jesus' authority ἐν τῷ ὀνόματί σου (in your name). The disciples protest because the exorcist does not follow "us."

Jesus' retort in v. 39 is an attack on the narrowness of the disciples. It is nonsensical to Jesus to think that one could act *in his name* (as a member of the faith) and turn right around and insult him.[16] Jesus continues his reprimand of the disciples in vv. 40 and 41, attacking their exclusiveness and self-esteem. In opposition to the disciples' narrow exclusiveness Jesus advocates a broad inclusiveness.[17]

---

15. Cf. Hans Bietenhard, "ὄνομα," *TDNT* 5:277.

16. Cf. W. Grundmann, *Das Evangelium nach Markus* (Berlin: Evangelische Verlagsanstalt, 1959), p. 197, who understands the meaning of ἐπὶ τῷ ὀνόματί μου in v. 39 in the sense of a confession to Christ. Cf. also Bietenhard, "ὄνομα," p. 277; Georgi, *Die Gegner*, p. 213.

17. ἐν ὀνόματι (v. 41) differs from ἐπὶ τῷ ὀνόματί μου which occurs almost as a technical phrase identifying one who confesses to Christ in 9:37–39 and 13:6 (see below, pp. 78–79). ἐν ὀνόματι does not carry such a narrow christological connotation. There is no descriptive pronoun or noun which would qualify its meaning. ἐν ὀνόματι ὅτι Χριστοῦ ἐστε must be translated "on the basis that you are of Christ" (a Christian). The addition of μου by a later scribe is caused by his sensitivity for the christological interpretation of ὄνομα in vv. 37, 38, 39. Thus, Jesus' broad inclusiveness in v. 41 even extends to someone outside the community who performs a merciful act for a Christian. That person also will receive a reward.

This same attitude of exclusiveness on the part of the disciples is reflected in their response toward the children brought to Jesus (10:13–16). Once again they place themselves in the position of determining who can and who cannot have access to Jesus. Symbolically, the children represent the people of humble position who came to the faith, an interpretation suggested already by 9:36, 37. Much the same as rejection of a child in 9:37 is a rejection of Jesus, likewise the denial of the children's access to Jesus in 10:13–16 is a rejection of him. As in the previous instance, the disciples present themselves as the final seat of authority for judgment on community membership. In the cases of both the frustrated exorcist and the rejected children Jesus sharply inveighs against the disciples' misplaced claim to authority and superiority over others and counters their narrow exclusiveness with his own broad inclusiveness. The evidence points unmistakably to the conclusion that the Markan disciples not only viewed Jesus as a *theios-aner* Christ but also display all the traits of *theios-aner* discipleship.

The Seriousness of the Christological Clash

The intensity and thoroughgoing character of the clash between the *theios-aner* and suffering Son-of-man christologies cannot be minimized. I reject the notion that one must wink at the christological seriousness of the clash between the disciples and Jesus. Anyone who takes that position has not read 8:27–33 very carefully. It is in that pregnant pericope[18] that the whole drama is focused.

The disciples in 8:29 finally recognize Jesus as the Christ. As we have shown, they understood this to be a Christ modeled after the Hellenistic *theios aner*. Strangely—at least to the reader at this point and, of course, to the disciples—no sooner has Peter evoked this confession than

---

18. Ernst Haenchen, "Die Komposition von MK VII 27–IX 1 und Par.," *Nov Test* 6 (1963): 81–109, has convinced me that Mark 8:27–9:1 is a Markan construction.

Jesus muzzles him (8:30). This silencing corresponds to the silencing of the confessions of the demons (1:25, 34; 3:11–12). Unlike Ulrich Luz,[19] I cannot see how this can be anything but a negative response by Jesus to the confession of Peter and the disciples. Nor can I join the commonly accepted Wredian interpretation that the silence was enjoined because the time of messianic revelation is only inaugurated with Easter. Even a quick reading of the Gospel proves this not to be the case (2:10, 28; 8:31; 10:46–52; 11:7–10; 14:61–62; 15:39).[20]

Following the silencing of the Petrine christological statement, Jesus introduces his own messianic declaration for the first time. He, as the Son of man, will suffer much, be rejected by the authorities, be killed, and then will rise again (8:31). Then, in perfect counterbalance to the silencing of Peter's confession, Jesus submits this statement as a public pronouncement ("and he said this openly").[21] It is Jesus' censoring of Peter's position and Jesus' unconcealed declaration of his own that produces Peter's rebuke. Jesus has no recourse then but to rebuke Peter. The sharpness and the intensity of this conflict is communicated in large measure by the antithetical parallelism built into the structure of the pericope. In reply to Jesus' christological query (8:27–28)

---

19. Luz, "Das Geheimnismotiv," pp. 23 ff.

20. Cf. T. A. Burkill, *Mysterious Revelation* (Ithaca, N. Y.: Cornell University Press, 1963), pp. 69–70, 128–29, 188 ff. Luz, "Das Geheimnismotiv," pp. 27–28, and Schreiber, *Theologie*, pp. 68–69, 77–81, 109, 201, contend that Jesus' full resurrected glory is revealed in his death. I find this to be an untenable position and will speak to its erroneous arguments below (pp. 124 ff.). Luz, "Das Geheimnismotiv," p. 23, on the other hand, has placed his finger upon a very significant breach in the Wredian position. The Son-of-man title is the only christological title in Mark that is not censored or cloaked in secrecy. Quite the contrary, Jesus publicly identifies himself with the Son-of-man title (2:10, 28; 8: 31–32, 38; 14:62); cf. also Norman Perrin, "The Creative Use of the Son of Man Tradition by Mark," *USQR* 18 (1968): 357–65; and his unpublished papers, "Towards an Interpretation of the Gospel of Mark" and "Christology."

21. Quesnell, *Mark*, p. 175.

(1) Peter makes a christological statement that must be suppressed (8:29–30).[22]

Jesus makes a christological statement that must be proclaimed (8:31–32a).

(2) Peter rebukes Jesus (8:32b).

Jesus rebukes Peter (8:33a).

(3) Peter is Satan, thinks things of men (8:33b).

Jesus is the Son of man, by implication thinks things of God.

Two of the key passages in this parallel structure are v. 30, the suppression of the Petrine confession, and v. 32a, the open promulgation of Jesus' position. Even scholars who do not view 8:27–33 as essentially a Markan creation identify these two passages as Markan interpolations.[23] What other purpose does Mark have in these two verses but to juxtapose clearly two conflicting christological positions, the *theios-aner* christology and the suffering Son-of-man christology?

Many advocating the Wredian position would argue that the Caesarea Philippi pericope only indicates a shift in

22. Ernst Lohmeyer, *Das Evangelium des Markus*, 15th ed. (Göttingen: Vandenhoeck and Ruprecht, 1959), p. 165, suggests that ἐπιτιμᾶν (rebuke) is the key word of the passage. So viewed, I believe it should carry the intense connotation of rebuke in all of its occurrences in the passage. Jesus' initial response to the Petrine confession then must be recognized as a rebuke and not a request to guard his secret, as the response is so often interpreted. The fact that the term is used by Jesus everywhere else in Mark (1:25; 3:12; 4:39; 9:25) as a term against a demonic adversary supports this position (note that Peter is also a demonic adversary in 8:33). One passage which is particularly illuminating and supportive is 1:24–25. In the synagogue at Capernaum Jesus is confronted by an unclean spirit who makes a christological confession: "I know who you are, the Holy One of God." On hearing this Jesus rebukes him and exorcises the demon. The parallel character of the two passages convinces me that Mark's understanding of the response of Jesus to the Petrine confession is analogous to the response of Jesus to the spirit's confession. Both confessions are rejected.

23. Cf., e.g., Erich Dinkler, "Petrusbekenntnis und Satanwort (Das Problem der Messianität Jesu)," *Zeit und Geschichte* (Bultmann festschrift), ed. Erich Dinkler (Tübingen: J. C. B. Mohr, 1964), pp. 127–53; Ferdinand Hahn, *Titles of Jesus in Christology*, trans. Harold Knight and George Ogg (London: Lutterworth Press, 1969), pp. 223 ff.; Georg Strecker, "The Passion and Resurrection Predictions in Mark's Gospel," *Int* 22 (1968): 427, 438.

messianic instruction to the suffering Son-of-man concept, which, like the former christological titles applied to Jesus, must remain obscure, unknown, and unpublicized until the resurrection. But this is the error of the Wredian position. The Son-of-man position is the one christological title that is not suppressed in the Gospel. Jesus identifies himself as the Son of man before the scribes and Pharisees in 2:10, 28. There is no attempt here to seal the lips of the scribes and Pharisees following these revelations. When the chief priests interrogate Jesus as to his messianic self-identity, Jesus adopts the Son-of-man title and imagery (14:61–62; cf. 13:26).[24] Similarly, the centurion makes his confession at the cross because he has witnessed the suffering, rejection, and death of Jesus. It is true that he calls him the Son of God and not the Son of man. But the critical point is that this confession is evoked only because the rubrics for the suffering Son-of-man christology outlined in the passion predictions have been faithfully followed: suffering many things (15:15–32), rejection by the chief priest and scribes and elders (15:1, 11, 31–32), and being killed (15:37, 39, 44–45).[25]

Additional evidence for the position that Son-of-man christology alone is intended for public consumption, while other christological positions must remain suppressed, can be found in Jesus' public declaration about discipleship and attitudes toward his messiahship in 8:34–38.[26] Jesus publicly pleads for suffering discipleship after his own model of suffering Son-of-man christology in 8:34–35. There is

24. So also Perrin, "Christology."

25. The one event that has not as yet taken place is the resurrection. But this is also significant. Authentic christological confession for Mark grows not out of the witness of the resurrection (cf. 16:6–8: no human confession is made as the results of the empty tomb), but out of the realization that the crucified is the Son of God.

26. The fact that Mark intends this to be a public declaration is underscored by the Markan introductory clause, "and having summoned the crowd with the disciples." Cf. Rudolf Bultmann, *History of the Synoptic Tradition*, trans. John Marsh (Oxford: Basil Blackwell, 1963), pp. 329 ff.; Schweizer, *The Good News*, p. 175.

no silencing of this christological position here or its corollary, suffering discipleship. In fact, Jesus apparently expects the disciples and the multitude to give due attention to his christological style and emulate it. In 8:38 Jesus makes a self-conscious connection between the future Son of man and his own public ministry. No injunctions to silence are to be found here. Quite the contrary, anyone who is ashamed of this public declaration (8:31–32, 34–35) and its implementation in Jesus' life will be looked upon with shame by the future Son of man (8:38). At this point failure to proclaim and live according to the dictates of this christological life-style would be a rejection of Jesus. Injunction to silence at this point would be incongruous. Voluntary silence, either by word or deed, is betrayal.

But the disciples, with their *theios-aner* christology and *theios-aner* life-style, reject Jesus' suffering Son-of-man christology and his call for suffering discipleship. Jesus tries three times in the passion predictions to persuade them of his christological position, but they either will not hear of it (8:32b) or cannot comprehend it (9:32). They persist in taking the human point of view and not the view of God (8:33). Like Paul's *theios-aner* opponents, they have become enamored of what attracts man: the miracle-working capacity of Jesus. They have ignored the most important aspect of Jesus, that which God ordains: his suffering servanthood.

The same results obtain when Jesus tries to persuade them to suffering discipleship. Again thinking like man, they want the glory, honor, the sense of self-exaltation, authority, superiority, and veneration from peers that the *theios aner* wants (9:33–41; 10:13–16, 35–45). Sacrificial discipleship (10:17–27) or discipleship without its tangible rewards (10:28–29, 35–40) is incomprehensible to the disciples. Even God intervenes to leave no doubt that Jesus' christological position has his blessing and to admonish the disciples to give careful attention to what Jesus has to say (9:7). But even this certification fails to alter their thinking.

When it becomes clear to them that Jesus intends to persist in his course, Judas joins the conspiracy against him (14:1–2, 10–11). The others signal their own complicity by their abandonment and Peter's impassioned abjuration of any association with or knowledge of Jesus (14:66–72). Peter's initial rebuke of Jesus' christology (8:32) is now restated in even more hardened and final terms. He is true to his character. Initially thinking like man in rebuking Jesus' christology, he thinks again like man in his final opportunity to change his position and affirm his belief in the suffering Son of man. He joins the Sanhedrin (14:53 ff.) in rejecting Jesus. The tears of Peter following this final and complete disclaimer are not inappropriate. For as he has been ashamed of Jesus and his words, so also will the future Son of man be ashamed of him (8:38).

What meaning could the presentation of such a christological conflict between Jesus and his disciples have for Mark? Why must he discredit the disciples and their christological position? Since there is no historical basis for a christological dispute of this nature having taken place between Jesus and the disciples, the only way to account for Mark's consuming interest in it is that it has some existential importance for the situation in his own community. But what kind of situation could have driven him to such polemical vilification? Does Mark provide us with any descriptive clues of his *Sitz im Leben* that could help us to find such an explanation? It is to this question that our attention now must turn.

III

The Markan Opponents

Clues to the import of the christological controversy in the Markan drama must be sought in Mark's *Sitz im Leben*. Since we possess no information about the Markan community aside from the Gospel itself, we must turn to it for insights about the *Sitz im Leben* out of which it emerged. The difficulty of finding material in the Gospel which provides us with a transparent and clearly defined picture of the community is monumental. For Mark's subject matter is not himself nor specifically his community but rather a narrative of the activities and teachings of the historical Jesus. To be sure, as the form critics have shown us, the material Mark has used probably reflects more the *Sitz im Leben* of the early church—as a result of the hermeneutical interests of the early church—than it does the *Sitz im Leben* of Jesus' time. But even though the material has been reworked so that it addresses the needs of various situations in the early church, one cannot always detect with confidence at which point Mark's material actually depicts his own contemporary situation rather than some previous *Sitz im Leben*. The magnitude of this problem becomes apparent when one reflects upon the fact that a unit of material could mirror the purity of its original *Sitz im Leben* in Jesus' life, or it could exhibit the tangled and altering effects of its accommodation to two additional *Sitze im Leben:* the *Sitz im Leben* of the early Christian community and the *Sitz im Leben* of the evangelist's own community. In such a state such material would contain a mixture of three different layers of tradition.

Obviously the implementation of redaction-criticism analysis of Mark offers an appropriate method for separating the layer of material reflecting Mark's *Sitz im Leben* from materials reflecting earlier *Sitze im Leben*. But where in the Gospel does one begin with such an analysis? Where can one begin his study with any assurance that he will arrive at the heart of the Markan situation and not be diverted by some peripheral issue in the Gospel? Further, how does one determine what unit of material most transparently depicts the relation of Mark's thought to the crisis in his community which necessitated the Gospel?

In the search for such a seminal and transparent passage the following principle provides appropriate guidance. Material in the Gospel which deals obviously and specifically with the post-Easter life of the church, rather than the pre-Easter events of Jesus' life, offers the most natural contextual and indigenous setting and chronological continguity to which Mark could append the specific *Sitz im Leben* of his own community. Therefore, where the hand of the evangelist can be detected in such material we can in all likelihood find the most transparent view of the specifics in the evangelist's *Sitz im Leben*.

This does not mean that clues to Mark's community situation cannot be detected in material that deals obviously with the pre-Easter Jesus. Certainly the evangelist may reflect his community's concerns in such material. But it follows logically that it is easier to detect such clues in redactional passages found in material that is clearly dealing with the post-Easter period, as one must ony sift through subject matter dealing with two *Sitze im Leben* (the early church and Mark's own situation) rather than three *Sitze im Leben* (Jesus' own time, the early church, and the Markan situation).

The largest amount of contiguous material that meets these specifications is Mark 13. Nowhere else in the Gospel is there an extensive section addressing itself to the post-Easter life of the church in such a pellucid fashion. James M. Robinson suggests: "The Markan apocalypse at times fits the events of first century history and of the book of Acts so completely that it seems to be history written in the form of a *vaticinum ex eventu*."[1] We turn to an examination of Mark 13 to see what insights it may offer us regarding the Markan community.[2]

An Analysis of Mark 13

That Mark 13 poses some difficult problems of interpretation is well attested by the number of scholars who have sought to grapple with it and by the diversity of the solutions that have been proffered.[3] Recently, the application of redaction-critical analysis to Mark 13 by several scholars has uncovered important Markan literary characteristics in the chapter, characteristics which I believe serve as clues to unraveling the mystery surrounding its composition. It is now apparent that Mark has given a four-part structure to the chapter: an introduction (1–4), a narration of events leading to the termination of history (5–23), a description of the collapse of the cosmos and the appearance of the Son of man in glory (24–27), and a commentary on the significance of the last events of history and a plea to watch vigilantly for the imminent appearance of the Son of man (28–37). Mark's hand is most visible in the formation of sections 5–6, 9–13, 21–23, 28–37. Particularly significant in these sections is the Markan imperative βλέπετε (give heed,

1. James M. Robinson, *The Problem of History in Mark* (Naperville, Ill.: Allenson, 1957), p. 61.

2. Leander Keck, "The Introduction to Mark's Gospel," *NTS* 12 (1966): 365, also asks "whether the *Sitz im Leben* of Mark's whole outlook is not reflected more clearly here than anywhere else."

3. G. R. Beasley-Murray in his book *Jesus and the Future* (London: Macmillan & Co., 1954), pp. 1–171, has given a full presentation of the history of the interpretation of the chapter, prior to the advent of redaction criticism. For important works since his book, see Willi Marxsen, *Mark the Evangelist*, trans. R. A. Harrisville et al. (Nashville, Tenn.: Abingdon Press, 1969); Erich Grässer, *Das Problem der Parusieverzögerung in den synoptischen Evangelien und in der Apostelgeschichte* (Berlin: Alfred Töpelmann, 1957); Lars Hartmann, *Prophecy Interpreted*, trans. Neil Tomkinson, Coniectanea Biblica: New Testament Series 1 (Lund, Sweden: C.W.K. Gleerup, 1966); Jan Lambrecht, *Die Redaktion der Markus-Apokalypse*, Analecta Biblica, no. 28 (Rome: Pontifical Biblical Institute, 1967); Rudolf Pesch, *Naherwartungen* (Düsseldorf: Patmos, 1968).

vv. 5, 9, 23, 33) which serves as a signal to the reader that he should give special attention to the issue under immediate discussion. Mark's punctuated ($\beta\lambda\acute{\epsilon}\pi\epsilon\tau\epsilon$) and repeated reference to messianic impostors in vv. 5–6 and 21–23 leads one to believe that these impostors have something to do with problems in Mark's church.[4]

Given these findings it follows logically that the place to begin searching for clues to the Markan *Sitz im Leben* in chapter 13 is with the sections 5–6, 9–13, 21–23, and 28–37. Mark's intense concern about messianic pretenders in his community is an appropriate place to initiate the search.

The Impostors in Mark's Community

Who were these impostors to which Mark directs his reader's attention at the outset (vv. 5–6) and prior to describing the coming of the Son of man (vv. 21–23)? In my opinion 13:22 is a particularly enlightening verse. Enlightenment from this verse comes to us not so much in noting and examining the particular titles given to these pretenders, however. Investigation of what the titles "false Christs" and "false prophets" mean for Mark or even for the early community in general fails to uncover any commonly accepted technical meaning for these titles at this point. The term *false Christ* appears nowhere else in the New Testament, save for the parallel passage in Matthew 24:24.

---

4. Cf. particularly on these points Lambrecht, *Die Redaktion*, pp. 67–297, and Pesch, *Naherwartungen*, pp. 74–243. Cf. also, Hans Conzelmann, "Geschichte und Eschaton nach Mk 13," *ZNW* 50 (1959): 210–21; Keck, "Introduction," pp. 365 ff.; Neill Q. Hamilton, "Revolution and *Mark's* Alternative" (paper presented to the Society of Biblical Literature, New York, 1970). Lambrecht and Pesch disagree primarily over the extent of Mark's literary creativity in the chapter and the character of the source or sources he used in its creation. Lambrecht argues that Mark, using material from Q, freely composed the entire chapter. Pesch follows the more traditional position, arguing that Mark built his composition around his use of an apocalyptic source, which he reconstructs in 6, 7b–8, 12–13b, 14–20a, 22, 24–27. I tend to view the source more like Pesch. I think Lambrecht's strongest point is in his advocacy of Mark's freedom to shape his material as he felt necessary. I would reject the notion that Mark felt bound to his apocalyptic source in any subservient way. Hartmann's attempt (*Prophecy Interpreted*) to find a pre-Markan midrash on Daniel in the chapter is unconvincing.

On the basis of a word study alone one cannot say much more about the term *false prophet*. In the New Testament *false prophet* turns out to be a convenient catchall term used by different authors to designate their opponents.[5] Thus, one is called a false prophet if he is a Jew (Acts 13:6; Luke 6:26; 2 Peter 2:1) or a Christian (Matt. 7:15; 1 John 4:1 ff.). One is called a false prophet if he makes the wrong confession (1 John 4:1 ff.), or if he makes the right confession but does not have the proper understanding of the law and Christian order (Matt. 7:15–23). One is called a false prophet if he performs signs or wonders which lead the elect astray (Matt. 24:24; Mark 13:22; Rev. 16:13; 19:20).

It is in the description of the activity of the Markan false Christs and prophets that we get a better understanding of the type of people the evangelist has in mind. Mark tells us that these impostors performed "*signs and wonders* to lead astray, if possible, the elect." The word *sign* appears seventy-four times in the New Testament but only sixteen times in combination with the word *wonder*. The term *wonder* occurs sixteen times in the New Testament, always in combination with *sign*. The combination of the two terms occurs fourteen times outside of the Synoptics. Nine of these instances are found in Acts (2:19, 22, 43; 4:30; 5:12; 6:8; 7:36; 14:3; 15:12). It is apparent that the terms have some special meaning for Luke, a meaning which is directly related to his understanding of Christ and the apostles.

There is a growing consensus among scholars that Luke has a *theios-aner* concept of Christian existence.[6] This is

---

5. G. Friedrich, "προφήτης," *TDNT* 6:855–56. Cf. also E. Fascher, ΠΡΟΦΗΤΗΣ (Giessen: Alfred Töpelmann, 1927), pp. 183 ff.

6. See Ernst Haenchen, *Die Apostelgeschichte*, 13th ed. (Göttingen: Vandenhoeck and Ruprecht, 1961), pp. 82, 100–1, 671, 676; H. Dieter Betz, "Jesus as Divine Man," *Jesus and the Historian* (Colwell festschrift), ed. F. Thomas Trotter (Philadelphia: Westminster Press, 1965), p. 126; M. L. Hadas and Morton Smith, *Heroes and Gods* (New York: Harper & Row, 1965) pp. 101 ff.; Helmut Koester, "One Jesus and Four Primitive Gospels," *HTR* 61 (1968):235.

apparent in the Gospel in his strong interest in the legendary details of Jesus' life, his intensification of the emphasis on the wonder-working ability of Jesus beyond that which Mark and Matthew portray, his replacing of Mark's *theologia crucis* with a *theologia gloriae*, and his presentation of the crucifixion as the unfortunate death of a *theios aner*. In Acts, Moses, Jesus, the apostles, and Luke's hero, Paul, are all identified by traits appropriate to a *theios aner*. Jesus is described as a man of signs and wonders (Acts 2:22). Moses is remembered as the producer of signs and wonders in Egypt and the wilderness (7:36). The performing of signs and wonders characterizes the activity of the apostles (2:43; 3:1 ff.; 4:30; 5:21 ff.; 9:32 ff.) and the persons they accredit by the laying on of hands (6:5–8; 8:4 ff.). And Paul—aside from Jesus, the greatest *theios aner* of all in the mind of Luke—is not only pictured as a great miracle worker (13:6 ff.; 14:3, 8 ff.; 15:12; 19:12; 20:7 ff.), but he is almost deified (28:3 ff.). Luke even creates a proof text for this signs-wonders (*theios-aner*) activity in the history of the church by citing the prophecy of Joel 2:28 ff. (Acts 2:19) with one significant addition. He has inserted the word *signs* to join the word *wonders* already present in the prophecy. Therefore, one can conclude that Luke has used the combination of terms *signs* and *wonder* the nine times they occur together in Acts to authenticate or identify *theios-aner* activity (2:22, 43; 5:12; 6:8; 14:3; 15:12). Luke's usage of the combination of the terms *sign* and *wonder* in Acts amounts to almost a technical expression for the description of *theios-aner* activity.

Before we examine Mark's use of these terms, two other instances of the use of them must be noted. In 2 Corinthians 12:12 Paul uses these terms with reference to a defense of his own apostleship in the face of an attack by members of the Corinthian community who have a *theios-aner* concept of christology and apostolicity. Their specific attack on Paul is that he fails to exhibit sufficiently the qualities of a true apostle, which for them is one who preaches powerfully, has great pneumatic experiences, and performs signs, wonders, and mighty works.[7] Finally, in John 4:48 the two terms occur in the context of the story of Jesus' healing of the official's son. Jesus states, "Unless you see signs and wonders you will not believe." Bultmann observes that in contrast to other places in John, the demonstration of signs and wonders mentioned in 4:48 is welcomed by Jesus to authenticate his claim to be the Christ.[8] The Signs Source, from which this particular story was borrowed, followed such an authenticating procedure in its own *theios-aner* christological apologetic.[9]

This study of the joint use of the terms *signs* and *wonders* in the eleven of fourteen nonsynoptic places has shown that this particular use is related to some form of *theios-aner* activity.[10] The evidence strongly argues that we should interpret their use in Mark as a reference to *theios-aner* activity. The descriptive clause "will show signs and wonders" pinpoints the "false Christs" and "false prophets" as *theioi andres*.

Luke's response to the Markan passage offers confirmation of this. Luke follows the Markan text of chapter 13 fairly faithfully, making alterations in the material primarily where historical conditions necessitate it, e.g., Luke 21:20,

7. Dieter Georgi, *Die Gegner des Paulus im 2. Korintherbrief* (Neukirchen-Vluyn: Neukirchener Verlag, 1964), pp. 225 ff., and James M. Robinson, "Kerygma and History in the New Testament," *The Bible in Modern Scholarship*, ed. J. P. Hyatt (Nashville, Tenn.: Abingdon Press, 1965), pp. 140 ff.

8. See Rudolf Bultmann, *Das Evangelium des Johannes*, 16th ed. (Göttingen: Vandenhoeck and Ruprecht, n.d.), p. 153.

9. See Robert T. Fortna, *The Gospel of Signs*, (Cambridge: Cambridge University Press, 1970) p. 41, 221 ff. Robinson, "Kerygma," p. 140, and Fortna (p. 41) account for the presence of the anti-Johannine attitude toward signs in 4:48 as owing to the evangelist's own redaction. The insertion of 4:48, according to Robinson, is John's way of sarcastically putting down this offensive *theios-aner* position.

10. Mark 13:22 and its Matthean parallel (24:24) are the only occurrences of the terms *signs* and *wonders* together in the Synoptics. Three occurrences of the combination in the New Testament (Rom. 15:19; 2 Thess. 2:9; Heb. 2:4) not discussed at this point do not suggest any reason to raise doubt as to the conclusion drawn. Didache 16:4 contains the combination of terms in a context similar to both 2 Thessalonians 2:9 and Mark 13:22.

24. His major alterations to the Markan text are in the form of complete deletions of significant portions of the text, specifically Mark 13:21–24, 32–37. It is not difficult to understand why Luke chose not to reproduce Mark 13: 32–37. Luke opposed Mark's "imminent" eschatology (cf. Luke 21:8). He had resolved the eschatological dilemma of the delay of the parousia in favor of a positive understanding of the church's role in the present history of the world.

There is an equally logical reason for Luke's deletion of Mark 13:21–24. He saw in Mark 13:21–24 an attack upon the *theios-aner* understanding of existence he favored. So he deleted the passage when he incorporated the Markan material.[11]

Turning to the description of the imposters in 13:6, one encounters the problem of interpreting the statement "many will come in my name saying ἐγώ εἰμι (I am he)." Perhaps the easiest solution to the identity of the "many" in v. 6 is to assert that they are Jewish messianic pretenders. Yet closer examination shows that the text of v. 6 does not allow such an interpretation.

The "many" who came "in my name saying I am he" are Christians, not Jews. The term ἐγώ εἰμι has been recognized for some time as a formal title for the Deity. In the Christian community it was understood as an identification formula for Christ.[12] In Mark, Jesus uses it on two occa-

---

11. Note that Luke reproduces a non-Markan saying (17:22 ff.) with a warning similar to Mark 13:21 ff. The non-Markan saying that Luke has used attacks apocalyptic speculation, which Luke opposes. But unlike Mark 13:21 ff. it does not attack *theios-aner* activity, which Luke supports. It is for this reason that Luke found the non-Markan saying consonant with his theology and used it, and found Mark 13:21 ff. incompatible with his theology and rejected it. Luke follows a similar practice in expurgating from Q the unfavorable attitude toward a *theios-aner* position which remains in the Matthean rendering of a Q passage (Matt. 7:21 ff.‖Luke 6:46; 13:26–27). See in this regard Ernst Käsemann, *New Testament Questions of Today*, trans. W. J. Montague (Philadelphia: Fortress Press, 1969), pp. 83 ff.

12. Cf., e.g., E. Stauffer, "ἐγώ," *TDNT* 2: 352 ff.; Erich Klostermann, *Das Markusevangelium*, Handbuch zum Neuen Testament, no. 3 (Tübingen: J. C. B. Mohr [Paul Siebeck], 1950), p. 133; Ernst Lohmeyer, *Das Evangelium des Markus*, 15th ed. (Göttinger: Vandenhoeck and Ruprecht, 1959), pp. 270 ff.; *Grässer, Das Problem*, pp. 157–58.

sions outside of Mark 13:6 to refer to himself (6:50; 14:62). Matthew specifically interprets ἐγώ εἰμι christologically in the parallel passage to Mark 13:6 (Matt. 24:5). In John ἐγώ εἰμι is one of the most frequent ways in which Jesus identifies himself.[13] It is clear that the "many" in Mark 13:6 claim a christological title for themselves.

What is contested by some is whether or not one can identify these "many" as Christians. The controversy revolves around the meaning of the phrase ἐπὶ τῷ ὀνόματί μου (in my name) when it stands together with ἐγώ εἰμι (I am he). Such a combination creates a contradiction in the minds of some interpreters, for how can one speak of Christian pseudo-Christs? To make this contradictory combination of terms meaningful a number of commentators exegete the verse in a less offensive fashion. Schniewind, Beasley-Murray, and Marxsen, for example, interpret the phrase ἐπὶ τῷ ὀνόματί μου not to mean "on the ground of" or "by the authority of my name" (i.e., Jesus' own name) but rather understand it to mean that the "many" use the name and title of the Messiah (i.e., that they are messianic claimants).[14]

Despite the fact that this interpretation is less offensive, its less offensive character in no way guarantees its accuracy. Quite the contrary, wherever one finds the phrases ἐπὶ τῷ ὀνόματι and ἐν τῷ ὀνόματι in the New Testament, each connotes a positive relationship to its referent. Naturally, the meaning of the phrases may vary to some degree according to the context in which they are found.[15] But in the New Testament, outside of the Synoptics, wherever ὄνομα carries a christological connotation in these phrases, the phrases are used either in reference to members of the Christian

---

13. Cf. Bultmann, *Johannes*, pp. 167–68; Eduard Schweizer, *EGO EIMI* (Göttingen: Vandenhoeck and Ruprecht, 1939), pp. 30, 111, 137–38.

14. J. Schniewind, *Das Evangelium nach Markus* (Göttingen: Vandenhoeck and Ruprecht, 1949), p. 167: Beasley-Murray, *Jesus*, p. 108; Marxsen, *Mark*, pp. 171 ff.

15. Cf. Hans Bietenhard, "ὄνομα," *TDNT* 5: 270 ff.

community or they are used by members of the Christian community as a mark of their faith and ministry. Within the Synoptics, except for Luke 24:47, the use of the phrase ἐπὶ (ἐν) τῷ ὀνόματι understood christologically never appears in Matthew and Luke independently of Mark. The phrase appears in Mark at 9:37, 38, and 13:6. Earlier we saw that its occurrence at 9:37, 38 revolved around an internal problem within the Christian community and was applied to those who claimed to be Christians but were not following the leadership of the Twelve.

The data are certainly impressive. Setting aside Mark 13:6 for the moment, nowhere in the New Testament, including Mark, is the christologically qualified phrase *in the name* used to refer to those outside the Christian community. There is no evidence of its being used for the purpose of identifying deceptive behavior or deceit on the part of "outsiders." Whenever it is used to assert someone's relation to Christ, that person is always understood to be a Christian. There is no reason why the same conclusion should not be drawn for its occurrence in Mark 13:6.

A number of scholars today agree with this interpretation, despite the fact that it produces an apparent non sequitur in 13:6, i.e., Christians identifying themselves as Christ. Taylor believes that the deceivers of v. 6 very possibly could be "false prophets who claim to be Jesus himself returning from on high."[16] Pesch believes they are Christians passing themselves off as the coming Son of man.[17] Grundmann contends that the appearance of people making claims to being the returned Jesus is possible within a Christian community stirred by apocalyptic excitement.[18] Schweizer and Schreiber also argue that there were people in the Christian community who made such claims by the

16. Vincent Taylor, *The Gospel According to Mark,* (London: Macmillan and Co., 1959), pp. 503–4.

17. Pesch, *Naherwartungen,* p. 111.

18. W. Grundmann, *Das Evangelium nach Markus* (Berlin: Evangelische Verlagsanstalt, 1959), p. 263.

authority of Jesus. They account for such a phenomenon as their being a result of the excesses of spiritualism in certain sections of the early church.[19]

I find the suggestions of Grundmann, Schweizer, and Schreiber to be close to the mark, particularly when viewed against Käsemann's very provocative insights on the character and ramifications of pneumaticism in the dawn of the church. Käsemann describes the early Christian community as a Spirit-directed community in which spiritualism (or enthusiasm, as he calls it) was rampant. Caught up in the fervor and ecstasy of their pneumatic experiences, these Christians sensed a total oneness with the exalted Lord. This sense of identity with the Lord by the church sometimes reached such completeness that the believer might even lose consciousness of the line of demarcation between himself as an entity and the Lord he worshiped. This peculiar characteristic of the pneumatic phenomenon was particularly evidenced in the charismatic leaders of the community, the prophets, and the like. As the plenipotentiaries of Christ, they understood themselves to be not only the mouthpieces of the exalted Lord, but also to a certain extent the incarnate vehicles of the Lord's Spirit.[20]

One does not have to look far in the early Christian community to spot specific illustrations of this pneumatic phenomenon. The Gnostics that Paul encountered in his congregations at Corinth (1 Corinthians)[21] and Philippi[22] are prime examples of Christians with this particular mindset. But we need not limit our search of illustrations to Gnostics. One of the best examples of this phenomenon,

---

19. Eduard Schweizer, *The Good News According to Mark*, trans. D. H. Madvig (Richmond Va.: John Knox Press, 1970), p. 268; Johannes Schreiber, *Theologie des Vertrauens* (Hamburg: Furche-Verlag H. Rennebach K. G., 1967), p. 142.

20. Käsemann, *New Testament Questions*, pp. 82–107.

21. See James M. Robinson, "Basic Shifts in German Theology," *Int* 16 (1962): 79 ff., for a discussion of studies on the Gnostic problem at Corinth.

22. Helmut Koester, "The Purpose of the Polemic of a Pauline Fragment," *NTS* 8 (1962): 317–22.

most appropriate for our present discussion, is the Christian *theioi andres*. Käsemann finds such a *theios-aner* perspective reflected at points in Matthew,[23] and of course Georgi has identified Paul's *theios-aner* opponents in 2 Corinthians as exhibiting this pneumatic phenomenon. The warning against Christians claiming to be Christ in Mark 13:6 can be easily accounted for if these Christians are *theioi andres*. In the midst of the intense rapture of their pneumatic experiences it is quite conceivable that they could have evoked such cries as ἐγώ εἰμι (I am he).

The results of our exegesis of 13:6 and 13:22 obviously point to two different facets of the same religious phenomenon.[24] The pretenders which Mark warns his reader against in chapter 13 are Christian *theioi andres*.

Mark's interjection of a warning against *theioi andres* arising in the time of the church has obvious implications for our study thus far. But we shall have to delay further discussion on this matter until we have ferreted out other clues Mark offers us in chapter 13 which point to the character of his *Sitz im Leben*.

The Suffering and Waiting Church

We turn now to clues Mark offers about his *Sitz im Leben* in 13:9–13. Earlier in our present discussion we noted that scholars have found that Mark uses βλέπετε (give heed) to draw attention to and outline his primary concerns with regard to his own community. It was this insight that led us into the study of 13:6, 22. It is this insight that leads us now to explore the evangelist's interest in 13:9–13 and

---

23. The *theios-aner* activity is attacked in Matthew 7:21–23 because it is not carried out under the rubric of "doing the will of my heavenly father." *Theios-aner* activity carries the blessing of Matthew when it is carried out under this rubric, as in the case of Jesus' activity and that of disciples who evangelize under his commission (Matt. 10:5–14). Cf. Käsemann, *New Testament Questions*, pp. 84, 103; cf. also G. Barth and H. J. Held in Günther Bornkamm, Gerhard Barth, and H. J. Held, *Tradition and Interpretation in Matthew*, trans. Percy Scott (Philadelphia: Westminster Press, 1963), pp. 162–63, 165–300.

24. Cf. Georgi, *Die Gegner*, pp. 224–32, 243 ff.

28–37, passages where he punctuates his remarks with
βλέπετε and passages recognized as clearly evidencing
Markan literary activity.

There can be little doubt that Mark finds himself and
his church in the throes of a persecution severely testing
the survival capacity of the faith. Even a cursory reading
of 13:9–13 produces this impression. Obviously, one reason Mark penned the passage was to comfort his reader
with the knowledge that Jesus anticipated the community's
plight and offers salvation for those whose faith survives
this trial by ordeal. But more than this is at stake. At
issue also for Mark is the assurance that the faith that
survives is authentic faith. That this is his concern is substantiated by a careful look at 13:10.

In 13:10 the church is admonished that "the gospel must
first be preached to all nations." In view of Willi Marxsen's
comprehensive study of the word εὐαγγέλιον in Mark (1:1,
14, 15; 8:35; 10:29; 13:10; 14:9) the clause *the gospel
must be preached* takes on profound meaning. Marxsen
argues that the term *gospel* serves in a periphrastic relation
to Jesus in the phrase *for the sake of the gospel* when that
phrase is in contextual contiguity to the expression *for my
sake* (8:35; 10:29; 13:9–10). Even more, in Mark's mind
Jesus and the gospel are synonymous. Jesus is not just the
preacher of a gospel. Jesus himself is the entire content
of the gospel which he preaches. Marxsen claims that this
is the meaning of "preaching the gospel of God" (1:14),
where "of God" is christologically understood. "Jesus is
the gospel of God." Therefore, Jesus calls for belief in
Jesus (the gospel) whom he preaches (1:15). There can
be no other Jesus (gospel), but the Jesus (gospel), which
Jesus preaches through the Markan narrative. That is the
gospel (the Jesus) for which one is to leave his relatives
(10:29). Furthermore, Marxsen claims that in Mark's view
when this historical Jesus is preached, he becomes present
in the preaching. The preaching of the gospel produces
the reality and presence of its contents (Jesus).[25]

25. Marxsen, *Mark*, pp. 126 ff.

Keck finds Marxsen's insights on the Markan interpretation of the word *gospel* suggestive but overdrawn. Even
if Mark used "for the sake of the gospel" epexegetically
for "for my sake," he contends, "this functional inter-
changeability does not mean theological identity or that
one could assume that for Mark εὐαγγέλιον makes Jesus
present." Keck believes that Marxsen's concern to show
the synonymous relationship between Christ and gospel
for the evangelist has been carried on at the expense of
"the characteristically Markan nexus between Christ and
the Christian, expressed by suffering ἕνεκεν ἐμοῦ." Keck
contends that if the term *gospel* were equivalent to Jesus
in 10:29, then Mark's need to use it at this point is puzzling.
Keck would prefer to see the phrase *for the sake of the
gospel* carry more of the connotation "christianity," referring thus to a movement rather than to Christ the person.[26]

I agree with Keck that the Markan preaching of the
gospel does not make Jesus present in any real sense. For
Mark, as I shall show subsequently, Jesus is not present in
any *essential* way, not even in the preached word. I agree
with Marxsen that the term *gospel* is an equivalent for
Jesus himself theologically. Jesus is the content of the
gospel. For Mark the gospel and Jesus are one and the
same. If Keck perceives Marxsen's exposition of the
synonymous relation of Christ to gospel as one which has
pushed to the periphery the basic Markan interest in the
relationship between the suffering Christ and the Christian
who suffers for him, I do not find that lacking in Mark
even when Marxsen's interpretation is accepted at full
value. A careful look at 8:35 ff.; 10:26 ff.; and 13:9–13
not only substantiates this but bears out an intrinsic
correspondence between all three passages.

A generation ago Friedrich Busch argued that Mark 13
was an explication of 8:34 ff.[27] The same could be said
of 10:23–30. Thematically, linguistically, and to some

---

26. Keck, "Introduction," p. 357.

27. Friedrich Busch, *Zum Verständnis der synoptischen Eschatologie,
Markus 13 neu untersucht* (Gütersloh: Bertelsmann, 1938), p. 48.

extent structurally there is a close connection between
8:34–9:1; 10:23–31; and 13:9–13. Linguistically all three
passages contain the phrase *for my sake.* It appears nowhere
else in the Gospel. Thematically the question of require-
ment for salvation is of vital concern. In 8:35 if one wishes
to save himself, he loses himself "for my sake and the
gospel." In 10:27–30 salvation comes from leaving everything, including house, brothers, sisters, mother, father,
children, land "for my sake and the sake of the gospel."
In 13:9–13 salvation comes to those who have endured the
trials and tribulations of witnessing "for my sake" and for
preaching the gospel before all nations. The consequence
of this activity is that brother will turn against brother,
father against child, and children against parents. The
one who witnesses for Jesus' sake and preaches the gospel
(Jesus) to the nations will be hated by all "because of my
name."

Moreover, I find it striking that both 8:34–9:1 and
10:23–31 stand contiguously to pericopes dealing specifically
with Jesus' instruction about the character of his own
messianic role. Mark 8:34 ff. follows immediately the first
passion prediction. Mark 10:23–31 precedes the third
passion prediction (10:32 ff.). In this way Mark has inextricably linked christology with discipleship. The linking
of the phrases *and of the gospel* and *the sake of the gospel*
respectively to the phrase *for my sake* in 8:35 and 10:29
is an attempt to bind up the gospel inextricably with the
person of Jesus and with the Christian's call to discipleship.

What Mark is concerned about is that one does not
separate discipleship in behalf of Jesus from the gospel
which for Mark is Jesus. That is, the term *gospel* qualifies
the type of Jesus for whom one dies, loses the world, and
risks the disintegrating of his family ties. Gospel is the
Markan Jesus, the totality of what Jesus lives and teaches
the Markan reader. The "my sake" which one gives his
life for must be consonant with the Jesus portrayed by the
Markan narrative. In this way discipleship and christology

are integrally wedded. The call to die for "me" is a call to die for the "me" of the Gospel of Mark.

The other striking revelation in 13:9–13, suggested by 13:11 and supported by evidence in the rest of the chapter, is the resurrected Jesus' absence from the life of the community of believers in its struggle in world history. The community functions without the active guidance of its Lord. To my knowledge Conzelmann was the first to point this out.[28] In 13:11 reference is made to the impartation of the proper confession on the lips of the believer in the hour of hostile inquisition. In assuring the believer that his apologia will be provided, Jesus makes no personal reference or allusion to indicate that he is the intercessory agent who makes the inspired defense possible. The only intercessory agent mentioned in the passage is the Holy Spirit. One can only assume that he alone is the counsel for defendants of the faith.

In citing the intercession of the Holy Spirit one must not assume thereby that the resurrected Lord is understood to be present also, consequently invalidating the argument for his absence. Such a conclusion, while suggestive, ignores the distinction which exists in Mark's mind between the Holy Spirit and Jesus. Mark conceives of the Holy Spirit in the Old Testament sense as symbolic of God's action in Jesus and in those possessed by it. The Holy Spirit's function in the Gospel is as the divine power that guides and directs Jesus (1:12; 3:22–30) and others (12:36; 13:11; 14:38).[29] This of course means that those possessed by the Spirit have established a harmonious oneness between the Spirit and themselves. But this does not mean that there is essential union between the Spirit and the person possessed. Nowhere in Mark is there any suggestion that Jesus and the Holy Spirit are identical. The Holy Spirit's possession of Jesus is in no sense to be interpreted

---

28. Conzelmann, "Geschichte," p. 211.

29. Cf. Eduard Schweizer, "πνεῦμα, πνευματικός," *TDNT* 6: 396, 401; Robinson, *The Problem*, pp. 29 ff.; Betz, "Jesus," p. 122.

as resulting in the loss of the distinctive and separate identities of the two beings. Reference to several key passages will bear this out not only in the case of Jesus but also for other Markan personae led by the Spirit.

One passage that is particularly instructive at this point is 3:22–30. The unforgivable sin in this story is not an attack on Jesus but an attack upon the Holy Spirit which guides him (cf. 3:22, 30). Thus in the story, and the principle of forgiveness which follows, a distinction is made between the vehicle of the Spirit (Jesus) and the Spirit itself.

Mark 12:36; 13:11; and 14:38 need to be cited in support of a Markan conservation of the separate identity of the Holy Spirit over against those who are guided by it. Mark 12:36 depicts David as being moved to a profound insight by inspiration of the Holy Spirit. Mark 13:11, as we have already noted, declares that the trial confessions of Christians are directed by the Holy Spirit. Similarly, while 14:38 is not an example of the guidance of the Holy Spirit in the lives of Peter, James, and John, it does imply that such might have been possible if these disciples had not been inclined otherwise.[30]

Our look at the Markan presentation of the Holy Spirit and its activity in the lives of the personae in the Gospel has produced important data. At no time, even in the case of Jesus, do the lines of identity between Spirit and the personae possessed by it become so blurred that the separate and distinct entities of each are lost. Furthermore, and quite significant in all these instances cited, the human persona is never the active agent but always the passive vehicle which permits the Holy Spirit, the active agent, to work through him. This is as true of Jesus (1:12; 3:22) as it is of other human personae (12:36; 14:38).

---

30. With regard to 14:38, Schweizer, "πνεῦμα," p. 396–97, states that the phrase "the spirit is willing, but the flesh is weak" is not a reference to Hellenistic psychology. The word *spirit* in this verse refers not to man but to God, the Holy Spirit.

Thus, the reference to the Holy Spirit's intercession in behalf of the Markan faithful (13:11) cannot be construed as an implied reference to the presence of the resurrected Lord. Moreover, the intervention of the Holy Spirit in the life of the church does not necessitate the assumption that there must be some initiatory activity of the resurrected Lord, whether on earth or in heaven, to make such intervention possible.

Luke apparently was unhappy about the Markan insinuation that Jesus played an inactive role in this period, thereby leaving it to the Spirit to guide the faithful. In his rewriting of Mark 13:11 Jesus is obviously actively involved in the affairs of the church. The Lucan resurrected Lord himself directs the believer in his defense against his adversaries (21:15).

Matthew does not alter the schematic character of the Markan passage in his incorporation of it, though he transfers it to another position in his Gospel (10:17–20). Yet, though on the surface it would appear that Matthew agrees with the thematic presentation of Mark, in fact he holds that Jesus is clearly present in the life of the church. One could never read Matthew 28:16–20 and think otherwise. Jesus, Matthew believes, has promised to be with the faithful always unto the end. For him the risen Lord is not only present in the congregation but rules her.[31]

Further evidence that the resurrected Lord is absent in the life of the Markan church can be detected in the Markan Jesus' admonition not to be led astray by claims of his presence (13:6, 21–23). Jesus forewarns the Markan reader that there will be claims in the community that he is present (v. 6). People will hear reports that he is here or he is there (v. 21). However, the reader is to recognize that these reports are nothing but false rumors to lead the elect astray (vv. 6, 22–23).

To appreciate fully the significance and extent of Mark's determination to dramatize the belief that the post-Easter history produces messianic imposters but not the resurrected

31. Cf. Bornkamm, Barth, Held, *Tradition*, pp. 131 ff., 142.

Lord, we must look more closely at the structural pattern
of Mark 13. Mark divides his material into two consecu-
tive yet different spheres of action. The first sphere (vv.
5–23, 28–37) deals with the last epoch of world history.
That is the human sphere of action with all its tribulations.
The second sphere (v. 24–27) depicts the cosmic plane
of action. In this section the setting is the supernatural
realm and the cataclysmic occurrences there. This careful
demarcation between the inner-historical and the transcen-
dental-supernatural arenas of activity sets chapter 13 apart
from the customary apocalyptic schema. As Conzelmann
points out, other apocalypses tend to cause the historical
plane of action to slide almost imperceptibly into the
future supernatural plane of activity. The one merges into
the other without any clear delineation between the two.
Mark supplies this line of demarcation in 13:24 by raising
the curtain on the cosmic, transhistorical scene only after
the curtain has fallen on the final tribulation to occur in
the world arena.[32] Thus Mark has carefully provided us a
frame for history and all the events which will take place
till its end. His point is that only after world history has
come to an end will the final collapse of the cosmos take
place and the Son of man make his appearance.

In his narration of the history of the world to its end
(vv. 5–23) Mark has framed it by the warnings against "the
messianic pretenders" which we have identified as *theioi
andres*. By introducing these imposters at the beginning
(vv. 5–6) and the conclusion (vv. 21–23) of his narration
of world history, Mark not only underscores the seriousness
of the threat of these people (nothing else in the course
of history after Easter draws the same emphatic warning),
but also suggests that this threat spans the course of history
from Easter to the end of the world. The church, Mark
admonishes his reader, must be constantly alerted to this
menace! These messianic pretenders will continue to crop
up to the end of history itself. Moreover, and just as

32. Conzelmann, "Geschichte," p. 216.

significant, by framing history with warnings against false representations of Christ, Mark demonstrates that the period of world history after Easter is the period for the appearance of false Christs in the life of the community (v. 21). It is not the period for the authentic appearance of Christ himself. This accounts for the absence in Mark of any positive clues for identifying the real presence of the resurrected Lord in history. No aid can be given for identifying the authentic presence of the resurrected Lord in the community because he is absent.

World history for Mark, as Conzelmann has helped us to see, is an extremely bleak and negative period, the time of suffering and persecution for the church, the time not of the resurrected Lord but his impersonators.[33] The resurrected Lord makes his appearance in the transhistorical cosmic period only after the cosmos itself has collapsed (13:24–27). For Mark there must be no confusion in the mind of his reader about the fact that the future after Easter portends two completely separate, theologically distinct, and nonconcurrent epochs.

Turning to 13:28–37,[34] we discover that Mark sheds more valuable light on his community and its problems. Apparently that community finds itself in much the same predicament as the servants in the parable about the absent master (13:34–36). Like the master of that story, the resurrected Jesus is absent from his community. Jesus' return as the Son of man (13:26) is anxiously awaited. Members of Mark's church are increasingly apprehensive about the failure of the resurrected Lord to return. Jesus had promised his elect that there would be some who would not die before the Son of man came and the kingdom had

33. Conzelmann, "Geschichte," pp. 210 ff.; cf. also Schweizer, *The Good News*, pp. 261–84.

34. For excellent redaction-critical studies of this section see Lambrecht, *Die Redaktion*, pp. 193–255, and Pesch, *Naherwartungen*, pp. 175–202. Both have marshaled convincing evidence that Mark is truly master of his material in this section. I am particularly indebted to Pesch for a number of the insights on the pattern and intention of Mark's thought in 13:28–37.

burst forth in full reality (9:1). The Markan community finds the generation to whom Jesus addressed this promise coming to an end. The Son of man has not appeared. Nowhere is there any evidence that the kingdom has come with power.

Mark, through the lips of Jesus, speaks to these concerns. He promises that the generation will not pass before the end comes (13:30). In fact, the members of Mark's community can be sure that the Son of man's appearance is close at hand when they see the events prophesied in 13:6–23 occur (13:28–29). Mark guarantees the dependability of Jesus' promise by citing the eternal truthfulness of his words (13:31).

Yet Mark warns his readers that they must not slip into a preoccupation with trying to work out a timetable for the glorious event. No such timetable exists. No one knows the exact time (13:35). Neither the angels nor even the Son know the exact time. Only the Father knows (13:32). Whatever the time, it will be very soon. The members must not relax their vigil, lest the Lord return and catch them sleeping. More than ever Christians in Mark's church must watch (13:37)![35]

Mark's Interest in His Apocalyptic Source

Thus far our attention has centered on the passages in chapter 13 (vv. 5–6, 9–13, 21–23, 28–37) which analytical study has suggested hold the best clues to the concerns of the evangelist and his community. Little attention has been directed toward the role played in the chapter by a

---

35. Schreiber, *Theologie*, pp. 111, 127–41, contends that Mark senses no such anxiety about the delay of the parousia as I and others have claimed. He argues that the parousia has no essential theological meaning for the believer. The parousia has meaning primarily for the unbeliever who discovers in the appearance of the future Son of man judgment upon himself and vindication of the faith of the community posited in the crucifixion and Easter. It is difficult to understand how Schreiber can ignore Mark's pronounced and anxious concern about the imminence of the parousia expressed particularly in 13:33–37. For Schreiber to argue that this passage has its expectation fulfilled, at least for the disciples and the believer, in Gethsemane and the cross is to collapse Markan eschatology into Johannine existentialism.

large body of material customarily identified as belonging to an apocalyptic source (vv. 7–8, 14–20, 24–27).[36] Obviously its incorporation into the composition serves some function which speaks to the evangelist's interest in creating Mark 13. No study of the chapter can ignore its presence or fail to explain its purpose.

Our investigation to this point leaves little doubt that the culmination of the events depicted in 13:24–27 occupies an important place in the evangelist's attention. His insertion of this passage is not just a case of the writer's having material lying around and seeking an opportune point at which to use it. Mark's selection and placement of 13:24–27 at its particular locus in his composition was carefully calculated. We have already seen this in our discussion on Mark's schematic structuring of the two distinct and nonconcurrent epochs of the post-Easter future. We have also noted that the evangelist is preoccupied with the return of the master of the community in 13:28–37, a return which for the evangelist needed not only to be stated with conviction but to be dramatically portrayed. For this purpose 13:24–27 became indispensable. Moreover, Mark's preoccupation with the future Son of man is not limited to chapter 13. We find his mind turning to visions of this future figure in 8:38—9:1 and 14:61–62. Since 8:38—9:1, in particular, is in a context carefully composed by the evangelist,[37] we have strong reason to believe that

36. Almost a consensus exists among scholars that the apocalyptic source Mark drew upon consisted of at least vv. 7–8 (with the exception of 7c and 8c), 14–20, 24–27. Pesch, *Naherwartungen*, pp. 203 ff., is among the most recent to advocate this position. I concur with the judgment. It is quite possible that vv. 12 and even 13b (so Pesch) may have belonged to the source; but with respect to vv. 6 and 22, I view them almost completely as Markan compositions (against Pesch), as the discussion has shown. Pesch, *Naherwartungen*, pp. 219 ff., 225 ff., himself admits that vv. 6, 12, 13b, and 22 have been so rewritten or rearranged or both by Mark to fit his purpose that they hardly resemble the original intent they had in the pre-Markan source.

37. Ernst Haenchen, "Die Komposition von MK VII 27-IX 1 und Par.," *Nov Test* 6 (1963): 81–109; also Norman Perrin, *Rediscovering the Teaching of Jesus* (Harper & Row, 1967), pp. 18, 185–91, and idem, "Towards an Interpretation of the Gospel of Mark," an unpublished paper. Perrin in "Interpretation" also argues for the Markan redaction of 14:61–62.

wherever such references occur in the Gospel, they reflect the deliberate redactional interests of the evangelist and not some unreflective accident of composition.[38] Mark's excision of 13:24–27 from his apocalyptic source and incorporation of the passage in his chapter serves both an epochal-descriptive and theological function. It acts as the pictorial representation of the cosmic-supernatural epoch in Mark's structuring of existence after Easter, and it dramatically fixes and limits the return of the resurrected Lord to a period following the end of world history.

If this is the purpose of Mark's use of 13:24–27, what importance did the rest of his apocalyptic material (13:7–8, 14–20) have for him? When one begins to assess the possible significance of 13:7–8, 14–20, one is faced with an enigma. The emphasis in these verses is such that they arouse and foster the very essence of apocalyptic mentality. On the one hand, they appeal to the apocalypticist's interest in graphic presentation of the diabolical character of the period leading up to the end of the world. For him it is a period pregnant with cataclysmic calamities and unmitigated, intolerable suffering of the elect. On the other hand, they appeal to the apocalypticist's preoccupation with the establishment of a timetable of events for this diabolical period. The apocalypticist's calendaring of the last events helps to reassure his community that it stands in the last days. This calendaring comforts the community with the knowledge that all is happening under the watchful eye of God, who will step in to bring this evil age to an end and inaugurate a blessed new age for the elect.

The apocalyptic mind-set which these verses engender is foreign to one's impression of Mark's thinking elsewhere in the Gospel. His interest in the future Son of man and his expectation of the imminent approach of the kingdom of God is indisputable. He is a thoroughgoing eschatologist. But at no other point in the Gospel does the evangelist lead us to believe that he is interested, as an apocalypticist

38. Cf. Lambrecht, *Die Redaktion*, pp. 179–90; Pesch, *Naherwartungen*, pp. 224 ff.

is, in either arranging a timetable for the apocalyptic schema or in highlighting the key events which act as signs to the reader by which he can mark the development of the apocalyptic process. Outside of Mark 13 the references to the parousia are few (8:38—9:1; 14:62). The only interest Mark shows in dating the parousia in these other passages is to assure the community that it occurs before everyone of Jesus' generation has died (9:1; 14:62). If Mark, before his composition of chapter 13, had had any inclination toward apocalyptic speculation, he certainly passes up some excellent opportunities for trying his hand at this at 8:38—9:1, 11–13.

Moreover, as we saw earlier, Mark's treatment of these apocalyptic passages in chapter 13 is not in the manner which would be expected of an apocalypticist. One would expect an apocalypticist to draw all the apocalyptic flavor he could out of such passages. One would look for him to link his material in such a way that the reader would become immersed in the unbroken escalation of the apocalyptic process, swept along as he read to the climactic end and the dawn of the new age. But Mark's arrangement of his apocalyptic material in chapter 13 creates no such effect. The Markan arrangement, rather than producing a continuous, accelerating apocalyptic process, tends to work against the unfolding of such a process and at times neutralizes the entire apocalyptic emphasis of his special apocalyptic material. The insights of Marxsen and Grässer help us to see this even more vividly. They both point out that Mark has intentionally slowed the apocalyptic process in v. 7 with the addition of "but the end is not yet" and in v. 8 with the insertion of "this is but the beginning of the suffering."[39]

To these examples of the rupturing of the apocalyptic process, Grässer, like others, adds the obtrusive character of 9–13 and 21–23.[40] Verses 21–23 are particularly indica-

39. Grässer, *Das Problem*, p. 157; Marxsen, *Mark*, pp. 172 ff.

40. Cf. Grässer, *Das Problem*, pp. 159–62, and Conzelmann, "Geschichte," pp. 217–20.

tive of this rupturing phenomenon. Verses 19–20 speak of almost insufferable tribulation (endurable only because of God's merciful abridgment of history), which is followed immediately by the parousia (vv. 24–27). The intrusion of vv. 21–23 destroys the continuity and sense of immediacy underlying vv. 19–20, 24. If one removed these temporizing and neutralizing effects of the redactional work of Mark, the apocalyptic material would burst forth in much clearer and stronger apocalyptic tones.

Why, then, did Mark draw upon the apocalyptic material found in vv. 7–8, 14–20 if he is not in sympathy with its apocalyptic interests? Conzelmann and Pesch present an attractive solution. They argue that our evangelist is faced with a heresy which propagates apocalyptic speculation about the termination of this aeon and the date of the parousia. According to their interpretation, the only way Mark could squelch the heresy was to take the apocalyptic material of his opponents and turn it against them.[41]

Conzelmann's and Pesch's reconstruction of the Markan problem in chapter 13 is unconvincing. If, as they claim, Mark and his community are so threatened by a heresy espousing apocalyptic speculation, then why does not Mark make some reference to this problem earlier in his Gospel? If chapter 13 provides insight into the problems which agitate Mark's community and so led him to write, then whatever is uncovered in chapter 13 as the problem besetting Mark ought to emerge as a recognizable, primary concern of the evangelist elsewhere in his Gospel. The danger of apocalyptic speculation is not an all-consuming problem for Mark in chapters 1–12, 14–16.[42] Consequently,

---

41. Conzelmann, "Geschichte," pp. 210 ff.; Pesch, *Naherwartungen*, pp. 219–35.

42. Pesch, *Naherwartungen*, pp. 240 ff., recognizes this fact, but it is not a problem for him. He contends that the problem of apocalyptic speculation had not arisen at the time that the Gospel was written. When it arose, Mark, Pesch claims, wrote chapter 13 as a response to it and slipped it into his earlier literary work (see pp. 48–82, 221–30). Pesch's argument on the later insertion of chapter 13 into a completed text is unconvincing.

there must be a better explanation for Mark's interest in apocalyptic material, an explanation that fits more exactly the concerns of Mark expressed elsewhere.

Willi Marxsen interprets Mark's use of his apocalyptic source from another vantage point. He believes that Mark has drawn upon the events depicted in the apocalyptic source because they offer a descriptive presentation of the plight of the evangelist's community at the time of the Roman siege of Jerusalem in A.D. 66–70. The evangelist's message to his readers, particularly those still in Judea, is to flee quickly to Galilee, where the others have fled, to await the imminent return of the Lord (13:14–20, 24–27).[43]

Marxsen's interpretation falters on at least two counts. Most conspicuous by its absence, in light of Marxsen's view of Mark, is a specific reference to Galilee in 13:14–20. If a flight to Galilee is what Mark has in mind in his use of 13:14–20, a redactional insertion of his favorite geographical spot, Galilee, would have been in keeping at the propitious point in the material. Furthermore, Marxsen fails to take sufficient account of the nature of the serious threat that the impostors in 13:6 and 22 present to the Markan community.[44]

There is a better explanation for Mark's use of the apocalyptic material found in 13:7–8, 14–20. Mark's church, as our investigation has shown, is caught in the throes of suffering and persecution because of its faith. The suffering shows no signs of easing. Rather, it shows every evidence of continuing until the end itself (13:9–13). The negative and disconsolate character of this time is aggravated by the fact that the Lord of the faith is absent from his community.

The time is even more consternating and disruptive because of the arrival of certain *theios-aner* Christians in the Markan community who have plunged the community into confusion. These pneumatic exhibitionists have experienced

---

43. Marxsen, *Mark,* pp. 166–89.

44. Cf. criticisms of Marxsen by Conzelmann, "Geschichte," p. 215; Keck, "Introduction," p. 366; and Pesch, *Naherwartungen,* pp. 28 ff.

such oneness with the exalted Lord that the demarcation between Jesus and themselves is lost in their own consciousness. Consequently, in the height of pneumatic experiences they are able to evoke proclamations which appear to others to be claims for being the returning Christ. For those Markan Christians desperately looking for the return of the resurrected one and unaware of the dynamics of the *theios-aner* experiences, the "claims" evoked by a *theios aner* in the course of his pneumatic ecstasies are misleading. They have been misinterpreted as personal claims to be the returning Lord.

Mark is faced with a two-pronged problem. Despite the inexplicable delay of the parousia and insufferable conditions of the time, he must convince his community to keep faith that the Lord is coming imminently. He must, on the other hand, expose the position of the *theios-aner* sojourners as a heresy which deceives people into thinking that the Lord has already returned.

Mark decided that the most convincing way he could do this was to frame a narrative of the period from Easter to the end of the world and the appearance of the Lord as the future Son of man. To establish this schema Mark needed not only his own skeletal framework of the two distinct, nonconcurrent epochs but also substantial narrative material which could fill out the features of this framework and create the appearance of an unfolding narrative of the end of world history, the collapse of the cosmos and advent of the parousia. To accomplish this task he drew upon his apocalyptic source. That part of the apocalyptic source that appears in 13:7–8 and 14–20 was particularly appropriate to his needs. First, the events these verses alluded to sufficiently approximated the events of the reader's own time (e.g., the Jerusalem war), so that a reader could identify them as events of his history. Second, their thrust and climactic movement, culminating as it does in a terminal event closing out world history, provided the historical overview and continuum his narrative required.

Mark's drawing upon this apocalyptic material was not
without problems. The nature of the material itself posed
the dangerous possibility that the reader would be carried
off by it into apocalyptic speculation. To prevent this from
occurring the evangelist had to find ways to blunt or neu-
tralize any apocalyptic speculation it might inspire. The
means he chose to do this was to insert the neutralizing
and retarding passages between this apocalyptically charged
material from his source. Thus at 13:7 and 8, as we have
already noted, after his source material draws attention to
cataclysmic events of the world which might normally be
construed as signposts for the end, Mark reduces the intensity and significance of such events by inserting his comments: "but the end is not yet" (13:7) and "this is but the
beginning of the sufferings" (13:8). Likewise, he interrupts
the accelerated thrust of his apocalyptic source by inserting
a brief description of the "acts of the church" between 13:8
and 13:14 and by interjecting the warning about the *theios-
aner* sojourners between 13:20 and 13:24. Finally, he reminds his reader that any attempt to discover a possible
timetable for the final consummation from his narration is
an exercise in futility. No one but God himself knows by
what schedule these events will occur (13:32). The believer must take no stock in apocalyptic speculation. The
believer's task is to bear up faithfully in the present period
of persecution (13:9–13), beware of the false christological
claims of the *theios-aner* viewpoint (13:6, 21 ff.), and dili-
gently watch, for the Lord's coming is imminent and may
occur when least expected (13:33–37).

Methodologically, this inquiry into why Mark wrote his
Gospel began with an analytical study of the interaction of
the key characters throughout the Gospel drama. That
study uncovered the fact that Mark has devoted his whole
narrative to staging a heated christological debate between
the disciples and Jesus. In this debate it was found that
the disciples hold intransigently to a *theios-aner* christology,
while Jesus argues adamantly for suffering-servant christology. Conclusions as to what import this had for Mark's

community were withheld until a better understanding of
his *Sitz im Leben* could be obtained from the one passage
where Mark's *Sitz im Leben* is most transparently revealed,
chapter 13. The findings of the analysis of chapter 13
have shown that members of Mark's church find their faith
strained to the breaking point by the insufferable conditions
of their time and the inexplicable failure of the resurrected
Lord to return. The situation has been exacerbated by the
arrival in the community of Christians of the *theios-aner*
perspective who offer a view of the Christian faith which
is far more attractive than the position Mark has been advocating.

The reason for Mark's giving central importance to the
christological controversy between Jesus and the disciples
is obvious. It is the same controversy which rages in his
community between himself and his *theios-aner* opponents.
Mark's greatest fear is that his community will reject the
"authentic faith" of Jesus and succumb to the heresy of his
enemies.

The best internal test of the accuracy of this reconstruction of the Markan problem would be to reverse the argumentative process to see if the same reconstruction could
be obtained. That is, the soundness of the position is verified if one can begin with an exegesis of chapter 13 and
work from that point back into the Gospel to arrive at
the same conclusion.

If such a course is followed, the exegesis of chapter 13
would result in uncovering the same clues to Mark's *Sitz
im Leben* as the clues obtained in the exegesis just under-
taken. However, when a study of Mark is begun at chapter
13 the significance of the *theios-aner* impostors for the
Markan *Sitz im Leben* cannot be immediately determined.
Were they a real threat or were they just a problem among
many problems the community faced in the last days? A
judgment as to their significance in the Markan community
could only be made after the entire Gospel was examined
and clues were supplied from it as to the seriousness of
this *theios-aner* threat.

Where one began looking in the Gospel for help in interpreting chapter 13 would be the key methodological issue. The soundest methodological procedure would be to seek help in understanding the concerns of chapter 13 in that section of the Gospel where the same concerns are most likely clearly addressed. This would inevitably lead one to 8:34–9:1. It is here more than any other passage in Mark that one finds the closest thematic correspondence to chapter 13, namely, the concern for suffering for the sake of the gospel/Jesus (8:34–35; 13:9–13), the promise of salvation to one who remains faithful to suffering servanthood (8:35; 13:13), the question of confidence in Jesus' words (8:38; 13:31), the discussion of the coming of the Son of man with angels in glory (8:38; 13:26–27), and concern for the arrival of the kingdom in power in Jesus' generation (9:1; 13:30).[45] It is not surprising that there is such close correspondence in the themes of chapter 13 and 8:34–9:1. The two passages have been shown to be two of the evangelist's most carefully composed pieces. Busch, as already noted,[46] argued that chapter 13 was best understood as an explication of 8:34 ff. Consequently, it would be a sound and appropriate methodological step to turn to 8:34–9:1 to find help for understanding chapter 13 in the context of the total Gospel.

Once the importance of 8:34 ff. to chapter 13 is established, then a logical question would follow. Can the issue which provoked raising the concerns of 8:34 ff. give us any insights into what provoked the need to address these same concerns in chapter 13? This line of questioning would lead one to recognize that 8:34 ff. is provoked by Jesus' controversy with Peter over christology. That insight would lead one back to the first half of the Gospel and thence to the last half to find that the focus of Mark's attention in

45. Lambrecht, *Die Redaktion*, pp. 137, 190, 210, and particularly 296–97, points out both the thematic and terminological correspondence between the two passages. He even speaks of a parallelism in thought between 8:31–9:1 and chapter 13. See also Pesch, *Naherwartungen*, pp. 171, 186 ff.

46. See above, p. 83.

the Gospel is on the controversy between *theios-aner* and
suffering christology and discipleship. With this information
in hand one could then see what meaning Mark's reference
to the *theios-aner* impostors in chapter 13 had for his community situation. The conclusion would be that the problem in the community is the problem in the Gospel: What
is the authentic understanding of christology and discipleship? By beginning an analysis of the Gospel with chapter
13 and moving back into the Gospel, the same reconstruction emerges as emerged by beginning with the characters
and then turning to the *Sitz im Leben* sketched in chapter
13.

IV

The Empty-Grave Story and Mark's Polemic

Two problematic parameters plague Mark in his effort to discredit the formidable position of his *theios-aner* adversaries. One of these engaged our attention in the last chapter: the *terminus a quo* for the resurrected Jesus' return to and reunion with his elect. In Mark's mind the resurrected Lord's parousia could occur only after the end of world history and the collapse of the cosmos. To rest his case purely upon personal conviction would have won no debating points. His enemies could counter with the rebuttal that Mark's perspective on the absence of the resurrected Lord from the community in no way proved the authenticity of his position. It only pointed to the fact that Mark had not arrived at the point of spiritual perfection in which, at the height of spiritual ecstasy, he could communicate with the Lord of the church—a point his enemies claimed they had already achieved.

Mark decided to set chronologically the fix for this parameter—and thereby establish the indisputable authenticity of his position—by creating chapter 13, in which the historical Jesus unfolds the history of the world from his time to the end. The effect of this prophetic vision is that Jesus articulates the Markan position, exposing all claims to his reappearance before the collapse of the cosmos as heresy.

The other parameter troubling Mark is the *terminus a quo* for Jesus' absence from the Christian community after the crucifixion. It is this parameter that engages our attention now. For Mark to argue that Jesus would not return to his elect until after the end of history would not completely inauthenticate the claim of Mark's opponents. They could argue that their experiences were not parousia experiences but continuing resurrection experiences. In other

101

words, our evangelist's *theios-aner* opponents could claim
with good precedent that they, much like the disciples,
Paul, and other early Christians, had experienced the manifestation of the risen Lord in their lives and continue to
experience his presence. How could Mark meet such an
attack? To take the position that resurrection appearances
could or did take place would have made his position
vulnerable to the impressive claims of his enemies. Yet,
in the face of the overwhelming evidence of tradition
could he deny or even ignore such a cardinal feature of
the early church's kerygma? How could Mark resolve such
a dilemma? The answer to this question lies in understanding our evangelist's verification of the resurrection and the
manner in which he terminates his Gospel.

For Mark, the fact and reality of the resurrection is
attested by the story of the empty grave. To state the
matter in this fashion is no glib rhetoric. Such a statement
speaks to a curious and puzzling phenomenon. Before
Mark there is no evidence that the early church ever sought
to verify its resurrection faith through recourse to Jesus'
empty tomb. Nor is there any hard evidence that the early
church ever knew of Jesus' grave's being empty.[1]

Furthermore, when Mark's use of the empty-grave story
is compared to the normative and traditional method of
attesting the resurrection, an even more puzzling phenomenon is disclosed. From Paul to John the customary proof
for the resurrection was the Christ epiphanies experienced
by the Twelve or other followers.[2] Mark's proof, by contrast, consists of an angel epiphany before three women.
That proof is hardly as convincing as an attestation of an
actual Christ epiphany before the disciples. This weak and
ineffectual character of the empty-grave story as a justifica-
tion for the Easter faith is graphically evidenced by the
reaction of Matthew and Luke to   Mark 16:1–8. Both

1. Cf. Hans Grass, *Ostergeschehen und Osterberichte*, 3d ed. (Göttingen:
Vandenhoeck and Ruprecht, 1964), pp. 139–84.

2. See 1 Cor. 15:5 ff.; Matt. 28:16 ff.; Luke 24:13 ff.; John 20:19 ff.;
Acts 2:32; 3:15; 5:32; 10:41; 13:31.

these evangelists found the grave story to be insufficient and even problematic as proclamation and convincing verification of the Easter event. Strikingly, although neither one agrees with the other as far as specific content is concerned, they do agree on one important point after they each incorporate their Markan source. Neither felt that what Mark recorded was adequate. Each recognized that convincing proof of the resurrection necessitated Christ epiphanies to the disciples (Matt. 28:16–20; Luke 24:13–53).

Why then did Mark deviate so radically from what was considered normative and conclusive in attesting the resurrection in the early church? Why did he choose, in preference to Christ epiphanies to the disciples, an angel epiphany to women? To what extent was this strange departure from the norm a deliberate innovation on Mark's part? To press the case further, to what extent can this deviation be attributed to Mark's attack upon his *theios-aner* opponents? To answer these questions we must examine the internal characteristics of the empty-tomb pericope and its relation to the whole Gospel.

The Empty-Tomb Story: Source and Redaction

No accurate assessment of the importance of the empty-grave story can be made without first separating Mark's source from his redaction. For only by isolating his source can one gain insight into its original character and function against which to make a judgment as to why Mark chose it and why he used it in the way he did. The most provocative and insightful redaction-critical analysis of 16:1–8 comes from Ludger Schenke.[3] According to Schenke, evidence of Markan editorial activity in the pericope surfaces immediately at 16:1–2. A close look at 16:1–2 shows that 16:1–8 could not have been connected to the burial story (15:42–47) originally. The burial narrative fails to support the conclusion that the interment was not completed.

3. Ludger Schenke, *Auferstehungsverkündigung und leeres Grab*, Stuttgarter Bibelstudien, no. 33 (Stuttgart Katholisches Bibelwerk, 1969), pp. 30–55.

Joseph of Arimathea's entire burial procedure—his preparations in the purchase of the linen shroud, the wrapping of the body in the shroud, and the sealing of the tomb with a stone—gives every indication that Jesus' interment was both complete and accomplished in accord with correct and respectful interment practice. Moreover, the picture of women coming to anoint a corpse which had already been decomposing for a day and two nights in that hot climate is difficult to accept, even if motivated by the most selfless piety.

The reference to the anointing plans of the women (16:1–2) must be traced to our evangelist. He introduced it to create a thematic link between two stories, a burial story and an empty-tomb story. In all likelihood the original story began with 16:2 and introduced Mary Magdalene, the other Mary, and Salome on their way to the tomb at sunrise. Mark lifted the names out of context and created 16:1 (the anointing motif) to act both as a thematic tie with the burial story and as an explanation for why the women returned to the tomb so early in the morning.

Such a reconstruction of the development of 16:1 also explains why one finds the awkward, redundant time references lying practically side by side in 16:1 and 16:2: "when the Sabbath was over" and "very early on the first day of the week . . . when the sun had risen." Mark created the time notation in 16:1 both to indicate when the spices were purchased and to specify with the notation "when the Sabbath was over" that the purchase was a prior act to the time of the women's arrival at the tomb, already fixed by the pre-Markan source (16:2, "very early in the first day of the week . . . when the sun had risen").

Schenke finds that 16:3–4 are redactional verses also. He reasons that the concern for removing the gravestone became a problem only when the evangelist decided to connect the burial story to the empty-grave story. The evangelist's source only spoke of the women's arriving at the grave and entering it. In fact, aside from the question of the removal of the stone in 16:3, the narrative is basically unconcerned about the stone. The text notes only that it was rolled away when the two Marys and Salome arrived. No mention is made as to how it was rolled away or by whom. No accompanying wonder, such as is found in Matthew 28:2, is narrated. Despite the fact that the removal of the stone is a prime concern to the women on the way to the tomb, discovery of its removal makes little impression on them. One could remove 16:3–4 and nothing appreciable would be lost from the narrative.

It was only when Mark made the decision to link the empty-tomb story to the burial story that concern over how the women were to gain access to the stone-sealed grave became a factor to be considered. Mark saw that his burial story described Joseph's closing the grave with a stone but that his empty-tomb narrative made no mention of its removal. He decided that this issue had to be addressed; therefore, he created and inserted the question in 16:3 and supplied the answer in 16:4. Impressive support for this explanation of the origin of 16:3–4 can be found in the close parallelism which exists between the syntax of 15:46 and 16:3, namely,

καὶ προσεκύλισεν λίθον ἐπὶ τὴν θύραν τοῦ μνημείου

τίς ἀκοκυλίσει ἡμῖν τὸν λίθον ἐκ τῆς θύρας τοῦ μνημείου.

In the final verses of our pericope, Schenke ferrets out two remaining redactional contributions of Mark. They are the angel's commission to the women (16:7) and the concluding remark about the fear-induced silence of the women (16:8b). In his interpretation of 16:7 as Markan redaction, Schenke takes basically the same position already espoused by a number of exegetes.[4] Mark 16:7 is a Markan throwback to 14:28, itself a redactional insertion of the evangelist. We have already looked in detail at Schenke's persuasive argument that 16:8b stands in tension to the thrust and intent of 16:8a and must therefore be viewed as redactional.[5] Schenke has successfully laid bare a pre-

4. See above, p. 47.
5. See above, pp. 47–48.

Markan empty-tomb narrative consisting of 16:2 (including the names of the women now in 16:1), 5, 6, and 8a.

The Empty-Tomb Story: A Translation Story

If this was Mark's source, why was he attracted to it and why did he edit it as he did? Half a century ago Elias Bickermann offered us a clue to understanding the Markan empty-grave pericope which very few commentators have embraced seriously. In a provocative article Bickermann sought to prove that Mark's story was a vestige of an early tradition which understood the Easter event as a translation of Jesus rather than as a resurrection per se. His reasoning followed the line that the empty grave does not prove the resurrection. He claimed that nowhere in the early Christian community is the resurrection proved by the disappearance of the body. It is authenticated only by the appearances of Christ. The point of the empty-grave story is to confirm the fact that Jesus is no longer in the grave. In this respect it conforms to the central motif and proof which lies at the heart of translation stories: the disappearance or absence of the corpse.[6]

While I disagree with Bickermann's view that for Mark the empty-grave story is not a proof of the resurrection, he is correct in categorizing the narrative as a translation story or "removal" story. Recently his valuable insight has been endorsed and pursued suggestively by Neill Hamilton. Hamilton contends that Mark used the empty-grave story because, as a translation story, it fit the peculiar demand of his Sitz im Leben.

Mark, so Hamilton claims, found himself in the midst of second-generation Christians just after the fall of Jerusalem. It was a time of crisis for the faith. With the death of the eyewitnesses to the resurrection, the new generation of Christians was cut adrift from the firm rootage and verification of the kerygma. Confidence in the faith was further weakened by the failure of the resurrected Lord

6. Elias Bickermann, "Das leere Grab," ZNW 23 (1924): 281–92.

to return to his community, a hope which was generated
by the original resurrection experiences. The community
desperately needed assurance of the legitimacy of its
Easter faith and reassurance that the hope in Jesus' return
was justified. Mark felt that the faith would in no way be
served by intensifying attention to the tradition of the resurrection appearances. The hope and survival of the faith
for him lay solely in the expectation of meeting the Lord
as the coming Son of man. The community's attention
must be pressed to the future and the parousia. Consequently, as Hamilton sees it, Mark used the translation
story as a substitute for an appearance story. He did this
to keep his community from being so distracted in the concern for shoring up the faith grounded in resurrection appearances that faith and interest in the imminence of the
parousia would be compromised, if not abandoned. For
this reason, Hamilton contends, the empty-grave story in
Mark's Gospel is better categorized as an antiresurrection
story.[7] In Hamilton's words:

> The most obvious thing about the empty tomb story compared
> to resurrection tradition is that it avoided the resurrected Jesus.
> It is as though Mark felt that Jesus' appearances to the church
> distracted the church from something more important; i.e., the
> Parousia. As we see in Paul, the presence of the risen Lord in
> some measure compensated for and made tolerable a delay in his
> return. Mark wished to eliminate that substitute for the Parousia.
>   Mark gave believers little encouragement for spiritual experi-
> ences of any kind. In place of the presence of the risen Jesus,
> Mark simply and strikingly affirmed his absence.[8]

How, then, was Mark to secure the confidence and faith
in the parousia if the cardinal proof of the Christian faith,
the resurrection experiences, was itself weakened? Hamilton argues that Mark chose to ground the faith in the
expectation of the future Son of man. He accomplished
this by convincing his community that the same Jesus

---

7. Neill Q. Hamilton, "The Resurrection Tradition and the Composition
of Mark," *JBL* 84 (1965): pp. 418 ff.; idem, *Jesus for a No-God World*
(Philadelphia: Westminster Press, 1969), pp. 60 ff.

8. Hamilton, *Jesus*, pp. 62–63.

whom the first-generation Christians knew in his public
ministry would return in the lives of the second-generation
Christians as the coming Son of man. Hamilton theorizes
that it was for this reason that Mark turned back to the
career of the historical Jesus. In the resultant schema
Jesus is portrayed as having two careers: the Son of man
who manifested himself to all in his public ministry, and
the Son of man who returns with power and glory in the
imminently approaching kingdom of God.

As a translation story, the empty-grave narrative serves,
Hamilton concludes, as a natural transitional narrative to
link the two careers of Jesus. In this respect Hamilton
views the two careers of Elijah as a precedent and an
important analogue for Jesus' careers. Elijah's first career
was as Old Testament prophet; his second was as John
the Baptist. As the two careers of Elijah are separated yet
transitionally tied by his translation, so also, says Hamilton,
are Jesus' two careers in Mark.[9]

Hamilton's position is very close to being correct.[10] His
formal identification of the empty-grave narrative as a
translation story is accurate, but his theological identification
of it as an antiresurrection story is too strong. It certainly
is not an antiresurrection story, for the resurrection is
forthrightly affirmed (16:6). The narrative is better interpreted as an anti-appearance-tradition narrative. I judge
it to be so because I see it as Mark's answer both to the
devastating claims of his enemies and the confessional
needs of his church.

Beyond question Mark had to conclude his work with
confirmation of the resurrection. But this was necessary
not because tradition dictated that he do so. Rather, it was
because to have concluded without some attestation to
the resurrection would have made a mockery of his position. Throughout his Gospel he has argued against the

9. Hamilton, "Resurrection Tradition," p. 420; *Jesus*, pp. 63–64.

10. He is off target, however, in his unconvincing argument that Mark
created the entire empty-tomb story; see "Resurrection Tradition," pp.
416 ff.; *Jesus*, pp. 58 ff.

grain of human credulity, much like Paul, that it is in suffering, humiliation, and life-giving love for others that one triumphs, that God's will is fulfilled. To take such a strong stand upon the necessity of the cross and then to ignore verification of the resurrection as a vindication of such a suffering life-path would have made his kerygma ludicrous. Allusions to the resurrection in the passion predictions and elsewhere (9:9; 14:28) were not sufficient. Mark had to have bona fide evidence that the resurrection did in fact occur.

Yet at the same time he could not use the proofs of the appearance narratives. To call on such proof would have played right into the hands of his *theios-aner* opponents. Once Mark conceded the reality of the narratives, his enemies could claim that their own spiritual experiences were completely consonant with these experiences—in fact, continuations of these Easter experiences. Mark's polemic against the legitimacy of his enemies' claims would thereby be severely, if not fatally, weakened.

How then could Mark authenticate the resurrection and at the same time maintain the integrity of his polemic against his *theios-aner* opponents? His answer was the translation story (16:2, 5, 6, 8a). The story was uniquely suited to his purpose. The next best thing to a Christ epiphany is an angel epiphany and an empty grave. Angels are accepted communicators of divine proclamation. Their integrity is unquestioned. An empty grave is a fairly good indication, barring the theft of the corpse (a factor plaguing Matthew, 27:62 ff.), that Jesus is redivivus. The two factors mutually affirm and support each other.

For Mark's interest the key verse in his source was 16:6. Once incorporated into his narrative, the elements of this verse took on special Markan connotations. In so doing they serve the Markan christological viewpoint admirably. In the Markan context the appellatives assigned to Jesus in 16:6 generate unusually rich associations. Identifying Jesus geographically with Nazareth locates him in Galilee, a region of immense theological import for Mark. It is the locus where Jesus proclaimed the authentic christology and eschatology (1:14–15; 8:27–31; 9:30 ff.) and where he was opposed by those advocating a *theios-aner* christology (8: 27–33). It is the locus of the parousia event (16:7).[11] Identifying Jesus as "the crucified one" not only attests to a biographical datum, but also in the Markan context alludes suggestively to the cardinal christological point of Mark's Gospel: that Jesus' messiahship can be defined only by crucifixion.

Both parts of the angel's proclamation to the women also have significance for Mark's kerygma. The announcement "He is risen" obviously certifies the fact of the resurrection and vindicates Jesus' commitment to suffering messiahship.

The announcement "He is not here. See the place where they laid him" states unequivocally that Jesus is no longer present on this earthly plane of existence. At this point one of Hamilton's insights is right on target: "In the place of the presence of the risen Jesus, Mark simply and strikingly affirmed his absence." The importance of the angel's words for our evangelist could not have been more sharply perceived. Jesus is absent! He is absent not just from the grave. He has completely left the human scene and will not return until the parousia! He has been translated ($\dot{\eta}\gamma\dot{\epsilon}\rho\theta\eta$)[12] to his Father. There he must await the time when the kingdom dawns in power (9:1) and he is reunited with his community (13:26–37).

---

11. In Mark, Galilee is a theological-geographical sphere where Jesus' public ministry occurred, where his parousia will occur, and where his ministry is carried on in the interim by the church. As such the boundaries are not limited to the geographical region of Galilee but extend beyond to include regions of the gentile world (see Ernst Lohmeyer, *Galiläa und Jerusalem* [Göttingen: Vandenhoeck and Ruprecht, 1936]; Willi Marxsen, *Mark the Evangelist*, trans. R. A. Harrisville et al. [Nashville, Tenn.: Abingdon Press, 1969], pp. 54–95; Johannes Schreiber, *Theologie des Vertrauens* [Hamburg: Furche-Verlag H. Rennebach K. G., 1967], pp. 171 ff.).

12. Hamilton, *Jesus*, pp. 63, 66, argues that Mark turned $\dot{\eta}\gamma\dot{\epsilon}\rho\theta\eta$ from a word traditionally referring to the resurrection into a word which connotes for him the translation (the raising or lifting up of Jesus). Thus each time the Markan Jesus speaks of being raised, he means translation, Hamilton claims, not resurrection.

This statement of the angel in 16:6 establishes the parameter for the *terminus a quo* for Jesus' absence from the human scene of action after the crucifixion. It is the effective check on any claims of Mark's opponents that experiences of Jesus are possible after the crucifixion. With Easter morning Jesus is absent! According to chapter 13, he will not be present again until his return at the end of the epoch of world history and the collapse of the cosmos. Anyone claiming that he is present before that is a beguiler (13:21 ff.).

The Meaning of 16:7

What, then, was Mark's purpose in inserting 16:7 into his empty-tomb text? The debate has been raging back and forth in recent years over whether 16:7 is an allusion to Galilean resurrection appearances or a reference to the onset of the parousia.[13] The advocates of the parousia interpretation press their convincing argument along the following lines. Mark 16:7, like 14:28, is a redactional insertion of the evangelist. If the evangelist had intended these two verses to refer to resurrection appearances, he failed to indicate explicitly that that was the case. Since he does not state this explicitly, one has no more right to assume that he has in mind resurrection appearances than any other

13. Among the advocates for the appearance position are Rudolf Bultmann, *History of the Synoptic Tradition*, trans. John Marsh (Oxford: Basil Blackwell, 1963), p. 284; W. G. Kümmel, *Promise and Fulfillment*, trans. Dorothea M. Barton (London: S. C. M. Press, 1957), pp. 77 ff.; T. A. Burkill, *Mysterious Revelation* (Ithaca, N. Y.: Cornell University Press, 1963), pp. 255 ff.; Schreiber, *Theologie*, pp. 42, 107, 109; Ernst Haenchen, *Der Weg Jesu* (Walter de Gruyter & Co., 1968), p. 546; Eduard Schweizer, *The Good News According to Mark*, trans. D. H. Madvig (Richmond, Va.: John Knox Press, 1970), p. 212. Among advocates of the parousia position are Lohmeyer, *Galiläa*, pp. 10 ff.: R. H. Lightfoot, *Locality and Doctrine in the Gospels* (London: Hodder & Stoughton, 1938), pp. 63 ff.; Marxsen, *Mark*, pp. 90 ff.; Norman Perrin, "Towards an Interpretation of the Gospel of Mark," an unpublished paper. Hamilton, "Resurrection Tradition," pp. 417, 421, and *Jesus*, pp. 58 ff., 64 ff., believes that Mark knew of the resurrection tradition of 1 Corinthians 15:5 and shows his awareness of it in 16:7; but Mark intends for 16:7 to be a contemporary word of assurance to his community that the parousia is imminent in Galilee.

possible visitation of the Lord with his community (e.g., the parousia). The aorist of ὁρᾶν, ὤφθη (he appeared) is the technical word used in the New Testament to refer to resurrection appearances, but the future of ὁρᾶν, ὄψομαι (will see) found in 16:7 and elsewhere in Mark (13:26; 14:62) is the term used in the New Testament for the parousia (so Lohmeyer).[14]

Since Mark is responsible for the insertion of these two verses and since Galilee has theological meaning for Mark in his own day, then one must not look back to A.D. 30 for the meaning of these insertions but to the eschatological concerns of Mark's time. Mark's community is distressed over the inexplicable delay of the parousia. It is Mark's task to reassure it that the parousia is imminent and hence that the community should not lose faith. He accomplishes this in part through the theologically loaded word *Galilee*. For to Mark and his community Galilee means the christological locus of the parousia. Consequently, the intention of the evangelist's insertions of 14:28 and 16:7, with their reference to the future event which shall take place after the future uniting of Jesus with the elect was both promised by Jesus and reaffirmed by the angel at the tomb.[15]

Moreover, according to Marxsen, 14:28 interprets 14:27. That is, 14:28 is a reference to the gathering together of the fractured community, scattered because of the crucifixion (14:27). That gathering together of the followers with Jesus in Mark's mind, Marxsen claims, could only be realized in the parousia, not at the resurrection.[16]

Finally, an important point for a parousia interpretation

---

14. Lohmeyer, *Galiläa*, pp. 10 ff. His case for the clear-cut specialized use in the New Testament of ὤφθη and ὄψομαι to refer to the resurrection and parousia respectively is not as solid as Lohmeyer claimed (e.g., Matt. 28:10 vis-à-vis 28:16 ff.). It is undeniable, though, that in two other occurrences of the future of ὁρᾶν in Mark (13:26 and 14:62) the reference is to the parousia.

15. So Marxsen, *Mark*, pp. 84 ff., 111–12, and Hamilton, *Jesus*, pp. 64 ff.

16. Marxsen, *Mark*, pp. 89–90. See also C. F. Evans, "I Will Go before You into Galilee," *JTS*, n.s. 5 (1954): 3–18, and Schenke, *Grab*, p. 46, who interpret 14:28 as a reference to the reuniting of the disciples with Jesus, but reject the parousia interpretation.

of 14:28 and 16:7 has been scored by Perrin. He has drawn attention to the fact that the two events uppermost in Mark's mind are the passion and the parousia. The significance of the passion for Mark requires no defense. The central role of the parousia is demonstrated by the special treatment Mark gives to his apocalyptic discourse. While placing it in tandem with the passion narrative, he is also careful not to place it in any subordinate role to the passion drama. He provides the discourse with its own introduction, independent of the passion thrust of the material surrounding the discourse. This special treatment of the apocalyptic discourse produces the effect that the Gospel really moves "to a twin climax of the apocalyptic discourse and passion narrative." The juxtaposition of the two narratives is Mark's technique of keeping in "tension the passion and the parousia."

The importance of and the intrinsic relationship between passion and parousia, Perrin argues, can also be seen in 8:27–9:8 and 10:32–40. In the case of 8:27–9:8 Mark has linked a proleptic experience of the parousia, the transfiguration, to the passion prediction. And in the intervening verses of this passage (8:34–38) he has shown that the positive experience of the parousia (8:38) is directly related to modeling life after the passion (8:34–35). Similarly, by appending 10:32–34 to 10:35 ff. Mark ties a passion prediction to the expectation of the parousia. At this juncture, too, he underscores the indissoluble connection between the two events through Jesus' admonition to James and John. A place in the parousia event comes only by living the way of the passion (10:37–40).

Everywhere in the Gospel, Perrin concludes, the movement is "through passion and resurrection to the parousia." He finds it "inconceivable that a climactic event explicitly and carefully referred to by *Mark* to take place after the resurrection [14:28; 16:7] would be a resurrection appearance and not the parousia."[17]

17. Perrin, "Interpretation."

The strongest argument against the parousia interpretation of 16:7 is the contention that any reference to Jesus' appearance to the disciples after the empty tomb would be understood by the church to be a reference to resurrection appearances. Certainly Matthew interpreted Mark 16:7 in that vein (cf. Matt. 28:10, 16 ff.).

Yet while this argument has its force, it commits the error of reading Mark according to tradition, without permitting the peculiarities of Mark to speak for themselves. The fact of the matter is that if one read Mark alone, without supplying the consensus of New Testament tradition, there would be no reason to assume that Mark meant 16:7 as an allusion to resurrection appearances. Aside from "possible" allusions to resurrection appearances in 14:28 and 16:7, there is no specific indication in the entire Gospel of Mark that such experiences did take place. No evidence can be found that the disciples or anyone else is privileged to the presence of Jesus after the crucifixion.

In fact there are clear indications that after the crucifixion Jesus is not only absent from the disciples but from all members of the Christian community. In an extensive discussion in the last chapter we saw how Mark makes it unmistakably clear in chapter 13 that Jesus is absent from his community after his crucifixion. He underscored the same point earlier in 2:18 ff. There Jesus was pictured as a bridegroom who would soon be taken from the wedding party (the Christian community). Jesus' conversation at the Last Supper leads to the same conclusion. In bringing the supper to a close Jesus announces that he will not drink again the fruit of the vine until he does so in the kingdom of God (14:25). The implication is that he will not be with the disciples or the company of believers in any real sense until the kingdom has come, an event still awaited at the time of Mark.[18] T. A. Burkill, in commenting on this

18. A. L. Moore, *The Parousia in the New Testament* (Leiden: E. J. Brill, 1966), pp. 136 ff. contends, as I do, that the occasion of the messianic banquet alluded to in 14:25 is clearly the parousia. He makes this judgment in part on the basis of the phrase *in that day,* which he interprets to mean the final day of the Lord, namely, the parousia.

announcement of Jesus, says: "But though the interim table fellowship of the elect would be 'without the Lord' in a physical sense, it was believed that it [the church] would be 'with him' in a mystical sense."[19] But Burkill's assumption has no support anywhere in the Gospel. In Mark, Jesus is not even present in a mystical sense, as our study of chapter 13 has pointed out. The fasting of Jesus in 14:25[20] is consonant and concurrent with the fasting in which the disciples participate after he is taken away from them (2:20). Fasting is in order because Jesus and his community are separated from each other, awaiting the kingdom. Jesus is present neither physically nor mystically. Again Hamilton's perceptive comment on 16:6 comes to mind: "Mark gave believers little encouragement for spiritual experiences of any kind. In place of the presence of the risen Jesus, Mark simply and strikingly affirmed his absence."

Marxsen's argument on the relationship of 14:28 to 14:27 has a place in this discussion. Marxsen contends that 14:28 interprets 14:27; i.e., 14:28 tells us that the community fractured by the crucifixion (14:27) will be united again after the crucifixion. In view of the relationship between 14:28 and 16:7, 16:7 must be judged to have the same meaning. It is the announcement of the gathering of the dispersed community and reunion with Jesus. Where is there to be found the one and only explicit reference to such a gathering of the elect in reunion with Jesus? Mark 13:26–27! At the parousia when Jesus appears with power and glory (13:26)! At the coming of the kingdom of God (13:26–27; cf. 9:1)!

One final note, drawn from Conzelmann, speaks to the strength of the parousia interpretation of 14:28 and 16:7. Conzelmann, as we saw earlier, construes the plight of

19. Burkill, *Mysterious Revelation*, p. 275.

20. That the point of Jesus' remark is that he is committing himself to fasting is exposed by Joachim Jeremias, *The Eucharistic Words of Jesus*, trans. Norman Perrin (New York: Charles Scribner's Sons, 1966), pp. 207–12.

Mark's community in similar fashion to Marxsen and Hamilton; namely, Mark finds himself caught in the "in-between"
time, between the rapidly fading time of the historical
Jesus and the anxiously awaited, inexplicably delayed event
of the parousia. The faith of the community is foundering
upon the unfulfilled hope of the parousia and the suffering
and persecution of its own time. More than anything else
it needs to have renewed confidence that it lived in the
historical continuum between the earthly ministry of Jesus
and his coming as the future Son of man. Mark sought to
establish such a continuum as an authentic principle of
faith. But his task was complicated by the fact that none
of the early creeds of the kerygma sketched such a continuum. They spoke of the death and resurrection but made
no mention of the parousia. Conzelmann claims that 8:38–
9:1 and chapter 13 represents Mark's attempt at building
this continuum.[21]

I would add to these passages 14:27–28 and 16:6–7 as
further evidence of Mark's attempt to create this continuum
for his reader. Both 14:27–28 and 16:6–7 exhibit the same
schematization of linking creedal statements to the promise
of the parousia: the death of Jesus (14:27; 16:6a), his
resurrection (14:28a; 16:6b), tied to his parousia (14:28b;
16:7).

As we have already seen, Hamilton follows a similar
line of reasoning in his interpretation of the significance
of the empty-tomb story. He argues that the grave story
is a translation story used by Mark as the transitional link
to provide this continuum between the two careers of
Jesus—his public ministry and his return as the future Son
of man. Picking up Hamilton's suggestion, one could then
argue that Mark's appending of 16:7 to 16:6 exposes the
rudimentary core of Mark's interest in this pericope and

---

21. Hans Conzelmann, "Geschichte und Eschaton nach Mk 13," *ZNW* 50
(1959): 210–11, and idem, "Present and Future in the Synoptic Tradition," trans. Jack Wilson, *JTC* 5 (1968): 31–32. Perrin, "Interpretation,"
makes essentially the same point when he argues that Mark has linked
the passion to the parousia to create a "movement through the passion
and resurrection to the parousia."

turns a translation story into a vehicle for establishing that continuity between the two careers of Jesus (his public ministry/passion and his parousia). To paraphrase Perrin a la Hamilton, everywhere in Mark the reader is led from the Jesus of the passion to the Jesus of the parousia through the resurrection (the translation) of Jesus.

The Point of 16:8b

In an extended discussion of 16:8 in chapter 1, I have already detailed my interpretation of the purpose of 16:8b. It is appropriate to review those findings and add to them insights derived from the present discussion. Mark 16:8b is the evangelist's final thrust in his vendetta against the disciples and his commitment to discredit them completely. By the time of the crucifixion event, the Markan disciples have turned their backs on Jesus, rejecting in toto his suffering path to the cross. They have blindly persisted in their *theios-aner* christology and discipleship. Their rejection of the crucified Jesus would not in itself totally denigrate them, as long as one assumes that they participate in the Easter experiences, where they supposedly would have been rehabilitated and commissioned as apostles of the church. That expectation vanishes with 16:8b. The sealed lips of the women deny Peter and the disciples' knowledge of the Easter event and its proclamation. The commission of 16:7 held open the hope that they could yet return to Galilee, the theological land of suffering messiahship and discipleship and the land of the parousia. There they could have turned from their apostate *theios-aner* position, accepted the Galilean theology, and joined in the reunion of Jesus with his elect at the parousia. That hope is shattered by Mark's concluding note to the empty-tomb story and the Gospel. The silence of the women robs the disciples of their apostolic credentials. More than that, it squelches Mark's opponents' claims of the disciples' participation in the Easter event and the experiences growing out of it, experiences so important for the validation of their own theological position.

V

The Opponents' Resurrection Story and Mark's View of the Exaltation

As we have seen, Mark chose to verify the resurrection with a translation story, rather than an appearance story, in order to authenticate his own christological position and avoid playing into the hands of his enemies' christological point of view. Yet even if this were Mark's reason for narrating the empty-grave story and for failing to narrate any Christ epiphanies after the resurrection, one might justifiably object that such a procedure would convince no one but Mark himself. For how could he really convince his readers or disarm his opponents by merely failing to narrate what the early kerygma stated had taken place? In defense of their position his opponents could easily claim that Mark either did not narrate the appearances because they were common knowledge (and therefore did not require repeating) or that he intended to do so but never completed his work. The evangelist anticipated this objection and has skillfully dealt with it.

The Transfiguration: A Resurrection Appearance

It was commonly believed in the early community that Jesus appeared to Peter and the other disciples (1 Cor. 15:5; Matt. 28:16; Luke 24:34 ff.; John 20:19 ff.). It seems to be the consensus of the early church that the appearance to Peter was the first Easter appearance and the key experience which ushered in the resurrection faith. Mark also knows of such an appearance to Peter, but as a preresurrection experience, not a postresurrection one (9:2 ff.). There is strong evidence that the transfiguration narrative contains elements of the original resurrection appearance of Jesus to Peter, which Mark took, reshaped into the transfiguration narrative, and predated so as to take place in the historical life of Jesus.[1]

Interpreting the transfiguration story as a resurrection story has met with strong objection.[2] The most formidable objection has come from those who point to its immediate context in the Markan Gospel (8:38—9:1, 11–13) and contend that it can only be viewed as a proleptic experience of the parousia.[3] That this interpretation is given to the story by its Markan context cannot be contested. But this does not necessarily mean that the story before its inclusion in Mark was narrated as a parousia story.

If the story were lifted from its present context and examined according to its own internal elements, it would satisfactorily pass as a resurrection story. The word ὤφθη (he appeared) is used almost as a technical word in the description of resurrection appearances. Describing the state of resurrection as transfiguration, though at variance with the synoptic accounts, is, nevertheless, consonant with a very early presentation of the resurrection. In this early view the resurrection, ascension, and exaltation were all

1. For a list of scholars holding this viewpoint see Rudolf Bultmann, *History of the Synoptic Tradition*, trans. John Marsh (Oxford: Basil Blackwell, 1963), pp. 259, 428. For more recent support of this view, see C. E. Carlston, "Transfiguration and Resurrection," *JBL* 80 (1961): 233–40; James M. Robinson, "Kerygma and History in the New Testament," *The Bible in Modern Scholarship*, ed. J. P. Hyatt (Nashville, Tenn.: Abingdon Press, 1965), p. 133; idem, "On the *Gattung* of Mark (and John)," *Jesus and Man's Hope*, ed. D. G. Buttrick, A Perspective Book (Pittsburgh: Pittsburgh Theological Seminary, 1970), pp. 116–18, 120; Margaret Thrall, "Elijah and Moses in Mark's Account of the Transfiguration," *NTS* 16 (1970): 305–17.

2. See, e.g., Ernst Lohmeyer, "Die Verklärung Jesu nach dem Markus-Evangelium," *ZNW* 21 (1922), 185–215; idem, *Das Evangelium des Markus*, 15th ed. (Göttingen: Vandenhoeck and Ruprecht, 1959), pp. 178 ff.; G. H. Boobyer, *St. Mark and the Transfiguration Story* (Edinburgh: T. & T. Clark, 1942); H. Baltensweiler, *Die Verklärung Jesu* (Zurich: Zwingli, 1959); T. A. Burkill, *Mysterious Revelation* (Ithaca, N. Y.: Cornell University Press, 1963), pp. 158–64; Eduard Schweizer, *The Good News According to Mark*, trans. D. H. Madvig (Richmond, Va.: John Knox Press, 1970), pp. 180–81; Norman Perrin, "Towards an Interpretation of the Gospel of Mark," an unpublished paper.

3. Cf. particularly Boobyer, *Mark;* Lohmeyer, *Markus,* pp. 178 ff.; Burkill, *Mysterious Revelation,* pp. 158-64; Schweizer, *The Good News,* pp. 180 ff.; and Perrin, "Interpretation."

one process. Jesus' resurrection was his glorification, manifested by his appearance in transfigured radiance (cf. Acts 9:3–4; 2 Cor. 3:18).[4] The presence of the cloud would be appropriate in the story in light of this early resurrection position. The cloud could very well serve as the vehicle for ascension (Acts 1:9; Rev. 11:12). On the other hand it could represent the symbol of God's presence or the abode of God's glory, a glory into which Jesus is received and transfigured.[5] The appropriateness of the presence of Elijah and Moses in such a resurrection story has been convincingly accounted for by Charles Carlston.[6] As prime examples of two Old Testament heroes who were translated into heaven, their presence attests to Jesus' being received into the heavenly realm.

Confirmation that the transfiguration could have originally served as a resurrection story can be found in 2 Peter 1:16–18 and in the recently discovered Gnostic gospels at Nag Hammadi. Bultmann contends that the author of 2 Peter knew our story as a resurrection story.[7] In his study of the Nag Hammadi documents, James Robinson reports that there is a close resemblance between the transfiguration story and the depiction of the resurrection event in the Gnostic gospels. Most striking is that in these documents the resurrected Jesus appears to his believers on a mountaintop in glorified, luminous form. Robinson conjectures that behind the Gnostic tradition is an early Christian tradition "suppressed in orthodox Christianity, and surviving in the New Testament canon only indirectly, at mislocated positions, having yielded the official position at the end of the gospels to the non-luminous human appearances." "Perhaps," Robinson concludes, "the appearance of Peter, because of its luminosity, ceded its position within the accepted period of resurrection appearances, and rather than

---

4. See Carlston, "Transfiguration," pp. 233 ff.; Burkill, *Mysterious Revelation,* pp. 160–61; Thrall, "Elijah and Moses," pp. 309 ff.

5. See Carlston, "Transfiguration," p. 238, and Vincent Taylor, *The Gospel According to Mark* (London: Macmillan and Co., 1959), p. 391.

6. Carlston, "Transfiguration," p. 238.

7. Bultmann, *History,* p. 259.

being simply lost, found a new location as the transfiguration story, which is clearly the same scene as that to which 2 Peter 1:16–18 refers."[8]

Mark's Purpose in Predating the Petrine Resurrection Story

It is now generally recognized by redaction critics that Mark is responsible for the present position of the transfiguration in the Gospel drama.[9] What was Mark's purpose in placing this resurrection-exaltation story back into the context of the public ministry? Recently a number of scholars have identified the transfiguration story as belonging to a *theios-aner* tradition.[10] The pre-Markan elements of this narrative consisted of 9:2–5, 7–8.[11] Its central motifs were (1) the transfiguration (glorification) of the *theios-aner* Jesus witnessed by two previously translated *theioi andres*, Elijah and Moses, and (2) the divine proclamation of the sonship of the glorified Jesus.[12] My contention is that this pre-Markan narrative was a resurrection story which belonged to the *theios-aner* tradition of Mark's opponents. The christological adversaries of Mark in all likelihood drew upon this resurrection experience of Peter, James, and John to serve as the foundation of their own pneumatic and christological position. That is, they argued that their experiences were consonant with and in the continuum of this experience and others which the disciples

---

8. Robinson, "Gattung," pp. 116–18. The Gnostic documents Robinson has in mind are *Pistis Sophia* 2–3; *The Letter of Peter to Philip* (CG VIII, 2); *The Apocryphon of James* (CG I, 1) *Sophia of Jesus Christ* (CG III, 4); and *Thomas the Contender* (CG II, 7).

9. See, e.g., Schweizer, *The Good News*, p. 183; Ferdinand Hahn, *Titles of Jesus in Christology*, trans. Harold Knight and George Ogg (London: Lutterworth Press, 1969), pp. 334 ff., 369; Perrin, "Interpretation."

10. Cf. Dieter Georgi, *Die Gegner des Paulus im 2. Korintherbrief* (Neukirchen-Vluyn: Neukirchener Verlag, 1964), pp. 215–16; Robinson, "Kerygma," pp. 133–34; H. Dieter Betz, "Jesus as Divine Man," *Jesus and the Historian* (Colwell festschrift), ed. F. Thomas Trotter (Philadelphia: Westminster Press, 1965), pp. 120 ff.

11. Verse 6 is a Markan addition emphasizing the disciples' lack of comprehension; so also Hahn, *Titles*, pp. 334 ff., Schweizer, *The Good News*, pp. 180 ff.; and Thrall, "Elijah and Moses," p. 308.

12. Cf. Georgi, *Die Gegner*, pp. 215–16.

had with the resurrected Lord beginning with Easter morning.

In predating the "cornerstone" experience of this christological position and making it appear in the public ministry, Mark undermines his opponents' kerygma. In effect what Mark has done in placing Peter's experience at this point in the Gospel is to expose the "truth" about the disciples' Easter claims. The experience which Peter and others were supposed to have had following the resurrection was not a postresurrection experience at all, but a preresurrection experience or an episode in the course of the public ministry which Peter, James, and John did not divulge until after Easter.

How could Mark possibly have scored his point, even if he wanted his reader to believe that the transfiguration was a preresurrection occurrence and not a bona fide resurrection experience of Peter? He did so by appending 9:9 to the story. Ever since Wrede it has been assumed that Jesus' injunction to the disciples to keep the details of their experience silent is the key to understanding Mark's messianic secret. The argument usually runs as follows. Mark 9:9 was introduced by the evangelist to help the reader understand why it was that knowledge of Jesus' divinity was not general knowledge before his crucifixion. Mark felt that Jesus intended to keep his messiahship secret until after the resurrection. Then it would be manifested to all.[13]

Such an interpretation of the Markan point of view is mistaken. Mark 9:9 is not an apologetic to explain the lack of public knowledge of Jesus' messiahship before the resurrection. Quite the contrary, it is a remark inserted by the evangelist in the service of a polemic against the disciples and their representatives in the Markan community. The point of 9:9 is to explain why an experience of Peter, James, and John during the public ministry, held by tradition to be a resurrection appearance, was mistakenly inter-

13. William Wrede, *Das Messiasgeheimnis in den Evangelien*, 3d ed. (Göttingen: Vandenhoeck and Ruprecht, 1963), pp. 66–69.

preted to be a resurrection experience. Mark 9:9 states flatly that Peter, James, and John were forbidden to talk about this public ministry experience until after the resurrection. After Easter morn they were free to discuss it with others. But then, according to Mark's logic, it was misinterpreted by their hearers to be a claim to a resurrection appearance.

Thus, Mark's positioning of the transfiguration narrative at 9:2 declares in unmistakable terms that the experience which his enemies prize so much as a Christ epiphany to Peter, James, and John, an experience upon which their whole christological and pneumatic position rests, was not a resurrection experience at all. It was nothing more than an event in the public ministry of Jesus which these disciples were forbidden to pass on until the Son of man was translated.

The insertion of the transfiguration story in the midst of the narration of the public ministry, however, serves more than just a polemical function. Through careful editing Mark turns his opponents' story into an apologetic for his own christological claims.

By thrusting 9:6 into this pre-Markan narrative, the evangelist changes an original insightful and reverential response of Peter into a reaction that portrays Peter as a dunce. By attaching the narrative at a point immediately after the first passion prediction and Jesus' discourse on suffering discipleship, Mark alters the original intent of the voice from the cloud. Before it was a part of the Markan context, the voice's function was to provide confirmation to the disciples that the *theios-aner* Jesus transfigured before them was the Son of God. In its present context the function of the voice is to serve as a reprimand to the obdurate and obstinate Peter (8:32–33) and an admonition to Peter, James, and John to give due attention to Jesus' teaching on suffering christology and discipleship. Where before the voice confirmed the *theios-aner* christology of Jesus, it now repudiates that christology.

Mark has used his opponents' story to affirm more than just his suffering christology and discipleship. By placing

the story in the context of discussion of the coming of
the future Son of man in glory and the irruption of the
kingdom in power (8:38–9:1), he has turned this resurrection story into a story of a proleptic experience of the
parousia. The result is two important effects—one obvious,
one quite subtle. The obvious effect is that he has given
dramatic emphasis to the parousia side of his passion-
parousia continuum, which was discussed in the last chapter.
The subtle and almost unnoticeable effect is the radical
change in the theological position on the exaltation of
Jesus, which resulted from placing the resurrection story
of his opponents in the context of the parousia event. The
pre-Markan story clearly describes the exaltation of Jesus
(his enthronement as the Son of God) as having occurred
at Easter. But with the placing of the description of the
exaltation in material dealing with the parousia, the event
of the exaltation has been shifted to the time of the
parousia. To put it another way, if the transfiguration
event is now a proleptic parousia experience because of
context, and if it is a description of Jesus' glorification
because of content, then Mark has postdated the exaltation
(enthronement) of Jesus to the parousia itself. Did Mark
intend this or is this an accidental by-product of his predating his opponents' resurrection story back into the public
ministry?

Mark's View of the Exaltation Event

It is a commonly held assumption that the early church
and the New Testament writers in particular understood
Jesus' exaltation as a fait accompli.[14] Certainly the support
for such a view of the exaltation is pervasive in the New
Testament. The early creeds found in Romans 1:3–4;
Philippians 2:6–11; Colossians 1:15–20; 1 Timothy 3:16; 1
Peter 3:22 lend their confirmation to it. Paul supports such
a position in Romans 8:34; 10:9 and in his use of the creedal
statements of Romans 1:3–4 and Philippians 2:6 ff. Matthew

---

14. By exaltation I mean enthronement: Jesus installed by God in his
unique status of Lord with all the powers and authority thereto per-
taining.

subscribes to this view by his reference to the power and authority which have been bestowed upon the resurrected Jesus (28:18-19). Luke alludes to the exaltation in Luke 9:51; 24:26, describes it in Acts 1:9-10, and proclaims it in Stephen's defense (Acts 7:56) and in the Petrine speeches (Acts 2:33 ff.; 5:31; 10:36). Hebrews depicts the exaltation as Jesus' ascension as the high priest into his heavenly sanctuary, and John holds that the exaltation occurred at the cross.

Yet when one turns to Mark he is surprised to discover that Mark is found strangely wanting in any positive and overt attestation of the exaltation as a fait accompli. In the nearest semblance to a kerygmatic creed in Mark, the passion predictions (8:31; 9:31; 10:33-34), there is no mention of the exaltation. Mark makes no declaration, as do Paul, Luke, and other writers, to indicate that the exaltation is an event which has already occurred (Rom. 1:3-4; Phil. 2:9; Rom. 8:34; Acts 2:33; 5:31; 7:56; Col. 1:15-20; 1 Tim. 3:16; 1 Peter 3:22). The evangelist cites no appearance of the exalted Jesus with his disciples as does Matthew (28:16 ff.), no description of the completed act of exaltation as does the author of Hebrews, and no description of the act in process as does Luke (Acts 1:9). Nor is there any suggestion in Mark that the exaltation took place at the crucifixion as is the case in John.[15]

In addition to this there is the rather unusual fact, already well discussed, that the resurrected Jesus plays no active role in the life of the Markan church. Like the bridegroom of Mark 2:18 ff. who is absent from his wedding party, the resurrected Jesus is absent from his church. As we saw, this point is emphatically scored by Mark 13. For Mark's community or at least according to Mark's christology, Jesus—resurrected, exalted, or what-

---

15. To argue this is to be guilty of reading into Mark Philippians 2:8-9 or the theology of John. Against Johannes Schreiber, *Theologie des Vertrauens* (Hamburg: Furche-Verlag H. Rennebach K. G., 1967), pp. 44 ff., I find no evidence that the cry of Jesus from the cross is a cry of triumph. We are given no hint of its content. It could have been a cry of anguish (15:34). Furthermore, the centurion responds not to the cry but to what he *sees* (15:39). See below, pp. 166-67.

ever—is absent. The Holy Spirit and the words of the
earthly Jesus (13:29) alone serve as support for the faithful
in the midst of the suffering life of the church.

The very fact that Mark nowhere refers to the exaltation
as a fait accompli, the failure of the passion predictions
to illuminate any allusion to the exaltation, the lack of any
encounter with Jesus after the discovery of the empty
grave, the lack of any mention of an ascension, and the
absence of Jesus in the life of the church certainly set
Mark's presentation of christology apart from the rest of
the New Testament. It raises the question of whether
Mark did not have an understanding of the exaltation
quite different from the normative picture one assumes
lies behind the whole New Testament. Is this possible?

Clues to the answer to this question must be sought in
the passages where Mark does discuss the exaltation—and
let it be quickly noted here that what has been said thus
far is not that Mark never discusses the exaltation of Jesus,
but rather that he never discusses the exaltation or alludes
to it as a fait accompli in his own time. Mark does in fact
make several references to the exaltation, but in all these
passages (8:38; 9:2–8; 10:37; 13:26; 14:62) the implication, if not the outright declaration, is that the glory of
Jesus becomes a reality in a future event—future not only
from the standpoint of the historical Jesus but also from
the point of view of the evangelist's own time. Exegesis
of 13:24–27 and 14:62 bears this out.

The Meaning of 14:62 and 13:26

The interpretation of Mark 14:62 produces no little
problem. The difficulty lies in determining what meaning
is intended when Daniel 7:13 and Psalms 110:1 are linked
together, since each carries a separate and distinct christological connotation for the Christian community. Customarily the Christian use of Daniel 7:13 has been to denote
the parousia of Christ in the "end-time." Equally definitive
became the use of Psalms 110:1 as the Old Testament
text by which the exaltation was alluded to and proclaimed
(Rom. 8:34; Col. 3:1; Eph. 1:20; Heb. 1:3; 8:1; 10:12;

12:2; 1 Pet. 3:22). The problem, then, in interpreting Mark 14:62 is this: Did Mark intend Jesus' reply to the high priest's question to be a prophecy of the exaltation following the crucifixion or a reference to his parousia as the future Son of man, or both?

J. A. T. Robinson, among others, insists that the use of Psalms 110:1 and Daniel 7:13 in Mark 14:62 is intended solely as a reference to Jesus' vindication and exaltation in contrast to the humiliation and condemnation brought upon him by his enemies. The mistaken identification of this Markan passage with the parousia, Robinson asserts, is caused by a false and inverted interpretation of the Son of man prophecy in Daniel, which is a description of an ascent of the Son of man into glory, not a descent.[16]

H. E. Tödt reasons, on the other hand, that if Psalms 110:1 and Daniel 7:13 were together intended to describe the exaltation, then the evangelist has done a very poor job of composing. For if he is describing the exaltation, the ascension of the Son of man to his throne, he has united the two Old Testament passages in the reverse order. The sitting at the right hand obviously can take place only after the ascension is complete, not the reverse, as pictured by Mark 14:62. Thus it is Tödt's contention, shared by a number of others, that 14:62 depicts the parousia-event.[17]

16. J. A. T. Robinson, *Jesus and His Coming* (Nashville, Tenn.: Abingdon Press, 1957), pp. 43 ff.; see also T. Francis Glasson, *The Second Advent*, 2d ed. (London: Epworth Press, 1947), pp. 63 ff.; Taylor, *Mark*, pp. 568–69.

17. H. E. Tödt, *The Son of Man in the Synoptic Tradition*, trans. D. M. Barton (Philadelphia: Westminster Press, 1965), pp. 37 ff., 285 ff. Others subscribing to the parousia interpretation of the prophecy in 14:62 are, for example, Erich Klostermann, *Das Markusevangelium*, Handbuch zum Neuen Testament, no. 3 (Tübingen: J. C. B. Mohr [Paul Siebeck], 1950), p. 156; Reginald H. Fuller, *The Foundations of New Testament Christology* (New York: Charles Scribner's Sons, 1965), pp. 145 ff.; Alfred Suhl, *Die Funktion der alttestamentlichen Zitate und Anspielungen im Markuse-vangelium* (Gütersloh: G. Mohn, 1965), pp. 54 ff.; Willi Marxsen, *Mark the Evangelist* trans. R. A. Harrisville et al. (Nashville, Tenn.: Abingdon Press, 1969), p. 84; Hahn, *Titles*, pp. 130 ff., 162 ff.; A. L. Moore, *The Parousia in the New Testament* (Leiden: E. J. Brill, 1966), p. 140. Johannes Schreiber, "Die Christologie des Markusevangeliums," ZTK 58 (1961):165 ff., and *Theologie*, p. 133, interprets 14:62 as referring to the unbelievers' witness to the power of Jesus in the parousia, a power and sovereignty bestowed upon him at the cross.

Norman Perrin suggests that our exegetical dilemma at this point is caused by the diverse interpretative uses which the early church made of Daniel 7:13. An examination of Mark 14:62a and Acts 7:56 convinces him that one finds in these two passages remnants of the earliest instance of the linkage of Daniel 7:13 and Psalms 110:1 in the service of a resurrection apologetic. The use of Psalms 110:1 to depict the resurrection is consequently qualified by Daniel 7:13, thereby representing the resurrection of Jesus as an ascension of the Son of man to the right hand of God.

A later interpretation of Daniel 7:13, Perrin believes, turned it to the service of a parousia apologetic by reversing the movement of the Son of man from an ascent to a descent. This interpretation he sees applied in Mark 13:26 and in 14:62b, which functions to shift the original resurrection-ascension meaning of 14:62a to a parousia emphasis.[18]

With regard to 14:62a, Perrin is certainly correct in arguing that in this particular passage the subject is delimited to the resurrection-ascension (an exaltation) and not the parousia as such. Elements of Daniel 7:13 in this verse are clearly consonant with the ascent movement of the LXX text. I break with Perrin's interpretation, however, when he argues that 14:62b is an entirely different use of Daniel 7:13 appended later to 14:62a. There is no question that 14:62b refers to an eschatological event, the parousia in particular. But 14:62b is not an instance of the use of Daniel 7:13 to refer to the descent of the Son of man in the way the parousia is customarily understood. Mark 14:62b directionally still depicts an ascent of the Son of man but chronologically fixes and qualifies the event as an eschatological event.[19] In this regard I am not as convinced as Perrin and Barnabas Lindars[20] that 14:62a

---

18. Norman Perrin, *Rediscovering the Teaching of Jesus* (New York: Harper & Row, 1967), pp. 173–84. Perrin's discussion on the evolution of the use of Daniel 7:13 appeared originally in "Mark 14:62: End Product of a Christian Pesher Tradition?," *NTS* 12 (1965): pp. 150–55.

19. Suhl, *Die Funktion*, p. 55, believes Mark is responsible for 14:62b.

20. Barnabas Lindars, *New Testament Apologetic* (Philadelphia: Westminster Press, 1961), pp. 48–49.

existed at one time independent of 14:62b and that only later, when connected with 14:62b, was its meaning interpreted as a reference to an "end-time" event. I believe with Ferdinand Hahn and Reginald Fuller that 14:62 was composed originally in one step and that it is a vestige of an early tradition of the Palestinian community which conceived of the messianic enthronement and the parousia as eschatological events belonging together.[21] Mark 14:62 is a declaration of the fact that the exaltation (act of enthronement) and the "end-time" appearance of the Son of man occur at the same time! Moreover, 13:24–27 substantiates this interpretation of 14:62.

Traditionally Mark 13:24–27 has been identified as the *locus classicus* for the description of the parousia, namely, the descent of the Son of man to the earth for judgment in the final eschatological event. Perrin certainly is one of the most recent advocates of this point of view. But Perrin and others not withstanding, careful examination of the evidence does not support viewing the movement in 13:26 as a descent. The data really argue more convincingly for the opposite position. The use of Daniel 7:13 serves to depict an ascent in Mark 13:26 in harmony with the original meaning of the Old Testament passage. More than that, 13:24–26 is, in fact, Mark's description of the act of enthronement! How can this radical interpretation of these Markan passages be substantiated?

In a number of New Testament creeds (particularly Phil. 2:10–11; 1 Pet. 3:19, 22; Col. 1:15–20) the glorification and the exaltation of Christ occur when the spirit-world powers are defeated and subjugated to Christ.[22] It is this defeat of the spirit-world forces which Mark describes in 13:25. Upon their defeat these forces behold the

---

21. Cf. Hahn, *Titles*, pp. 130–31; Fuller, *Foundations*, pp. 145 ff. Hahn's point that the two events are made one by the link word ὄψεσθε is an accurate insight (p. 163)—an insight also espoused by J. A. T. Robinson, *Jesus*, p. 51, though Robinson identified the event as the resurrection-exaltation and not the parousia.

22. See Eduard Schweizer, *Lordship and Discipleship*, 1st Eng. ed. (Naperville, Ill.: Alec R. Allenson, 1960), pp. 63, 66–67, 75–76. It is striking that after the reference to the defeat of Satan in John 12:31, reference to the exaltation of Jesus follows (12:32).

Son of man enthroned in all his glory and power (13:26). That it is the powers that behold the exaltation process is confirmed by the fact that the subject of ὄψονται (they will see) can be none other than the powers which have just been defeated.[23] There is nothing else to which the subject of ὄψονται can refer. The scene of 13:24–26 is restricted completely to the heavenly, supernatural realm. The participants are limited to the spirit-world forces and the Son of man. Nowhere is there even the slightest hint that there might be spectators of the scene observing from the earthly, human plane. The curtain on the earthly plane of existence fell in 13:24a, as we saw in our discussion in chapter 3.[24] The arena of 13:24–26 is exclusively that of the cosmic-supernatural. Human personae are not mentioned until the conclusion of the enthronement scene, *after* the spirit-world forces have witnessed the Son of man coming in the clouds, enthroned with great power and glory. Then it is that the elect, gathered together by the angels sent out by the enthroned Lord, are united with him (13:27). The direction of movement in 13:26 is consonant with the original meaning of Daniel 7:13. Mark 13:24–26 describes the ascent of the translated Jesus (16:6) to enthronement as the Son of man in the final eschatological event. Mark 13:27 describes the gathering of the scattered Christian community and its reunion with its now exalted Lord.

By their rendering of the Markan text, Matthew and Luke are responsible for clouding the issue in Mark 13:24–27 and causing many commentators to read a descent interpretation in Mark 13:26. In Matthew 24:29–31 and Luke 21:25–28 the participants in the final cosmic scene are not restricted to the spirit-world forces, as they are in Mark.

---

23. Commentators have usually interpreted the subject of ὄψονται as an indefinite, impersonal subject and have thought the implicit subject to be variously all men, the elect, or Jesus' enemies, among others. See Rudolf Pesch, *Naherwartungen* (Düsseldorf: Patmos, 1968), p. 167 for a discussion of the problem. There is no reason why such forced explanations must be sought outside the immediate text when the *fallen powers* serve as a natural, implicit subject of the verb.

24. See p. 88.

In Matthew (24:30) it apparently is the tribes of the earth that see Jesus coming on the clouds of heaven and not necessarily the fallen powers. Matthew's inserting of this new element in the Markan drama between the reference to the fallen powers and the verb ὄψονται alters the entire sense of the passage. The Matthean scene, depicting the tribes seeing the Son of man coming, turns a Markan ascent to enthronement into a Matthean descent to the earth.

In the Lucan version the scene restricted in Mark to the cosmic realm now becomes a universal scene portraying the dissolution of the heavens and the earth and describing the dire plight of nations and men (21:25–26). This insertion of special Lucan material also obscures the Markan meaning of the verb ὄψονται. By including the reaction of "nations" and "men" to the holocaust prior to the Markan references to the fall of the powers and the observation of the coming Son of man, Luke leaves the meaning ambiguous as to whether the subject of ὄψονται is the nations, men, or powers, or all three. It is natural to read the Markan scene in Luke's rewriting as a descent to earth rather than an ascent to enthronement. As a result, exegetes have been tempted to read the Lucan interpretation back into Mark.

Our analysis of 13:26 further confirms the interpretation of 14:62 suggested by Hahn and Fuller. In fact 13:24–26 serves to fix the interpretation of 14:62. The Markan reader knows that 14:62 is a reference to the final eschatological enthronement event, for by the time he reaches 14:62 he has already been informed by the evangelist (13:24–26) what the temporal fix for that event is.

The Early Palestinian Church, the Apocalypse of Peter, and the Enthronement Event

The view that Mark did not consider Jesus to be exalted or enthroned until the final "end-time" event runs counter to all other interpretations of Mark. Is there any evidence aside from Mark that would suggest that Mark was not unique in this respect? The early Palestinian community appears to have held the same view. Ferdinand Hahn

and Reginald Fuller reconstruct the *Sitz im Leben* of
that community as follows.[25] In the beginning the Palestinian church, while built solidly. upon a resurrection
faith, did not perceive of Jesus' being exalted to a position
of power and authority on Easter morn. Rather, it looked
upon the resurrection as only the beginning event in the
eschatological process which would reach its fruition in
the parousia. Jesus, according to this view, though translated to heaven at the resurrection, remains inactive, waiting in the wings, as it were, until the final act, the parousia,
when he emerges again, receives his full power and glory,
and is reunited with his community.

The situation was extremely bleak for the community
during this period. Separated from their Lord, these
Palestinian Christians found themselves in a cruel period
of suffering and misery while evil forces still abounded
in the world. Although they believed that the curtain on
the last eschatological act had risen with Jesus' resurrection, they recognized that realization of salvation for them
would not be possible until the final consummation when
Jesus returned triumphantly, enthroned with power and
glory. These early Christians, forced to live without their
Lord in the interim, compensated for the loss of his presence by reflecting on his earthly message of salvation and
call and by living in anticipation of his return. Their most
important possession was the gift of the Spirit[26] which both
sustained and assured them that the eschatological drama
was in truth in process.

Since the interval between the resurrection and the

25. Hahn, *Titles*, pp. 92–102, 129 ff.; Fuller, *Foundations*, pp. 145 ff.,
185–86.

26. This gift of the Spirit, according to Hahn (*Titles*, pp. 98–99), was
nothing more than a "substitute gift" to replace the loss of Jesus' presence
in the life of the community. The early Palestinian church did not make
any connection between the possession of the Spirit and Jesus' heavenly
activity. This connection was drawn only later when the church conceived of Jesus' functioning in the interim as one fully exalted, actively
involved in the life of the church. Excellent representative examples
of these two views can be found in Mark 13:11 (the early view) and
Luke 21:15 (the later view), the Lucan parallel to the Markan passage.

exaltation was only a transition period, of negative value, it had no importance for the Palestinian church in its christological-soteriological frame of reference. Consequently the church saw no need to speculate as to what Jesus' function and status were during the interval. Only after some lapse of time, the inexplicable delay of the parousia, and the spread of the gospel in the Hellenistic world did the Christians begin to give more and more positive content to Jesus' role in the interim. It was then, through the help of Psalms 110:1, that Christian reflection arrived at the position that Jesus' exaltation had actually occurred at the resurrection and that the Lord was indeed present in the life of his church.[27]

Hahn and Fuller have pieced together this early Palestinian tradition through the help of what they believe are remnants of the tradition in a number of New Testament passages. Hahn, who specifically identifies the larger number of these passages, finds these remnants in Matthew 25:1 ff.; Mark 2:18 ff.; 3:28–29; 13:1–37 (particularly vv. 9–13); 14:61–62; Acts 1:9–11; 3:20, 21a. Key passages in this group in Hahn's analysis are Mark 2:18–20; 13:9b; 14:61–62; Acts 3:20, 21a. It is important for our study to look more closely at how Hahn sees these various passages profiling this Palestinian position.

Against Haenchen[28] and in support of Ulrich Wilckens,[29] Hahn interprets Acts 3:20, 21a to be a piece of an old tradition, of Semitic origin, which speaks of Jesus as a

---

27. Schweizer, *Lordship*, p. 57; Eduard Schweizer, "Die theologische Leistung des Markus," *EvTh* 24 (1964): 10 ff., contends that Acts 2:36, which he insists goes back to the Palestinian church, is refutation enough against the claim that the Palestinian church would have had the kind of theology Hahn and Fuller attribute to it. Hahn, *Titles*, pp. 100, 106–7, and Fuller, *Foundations*, pp. 184 ff., however, ascribe Acts 2:36 and its inherent theology not to a Palestinian community but to a Hellenistic Jewish community which has arrived at the position that Jesus was exalted to lordship at his resurrection.

28. Ernst Haenchen, *Die Apostelgeschichte*, 13th ed. (Göttingen: Vandenhoeck and Ruprecht, 1961), pp. 170 ff.

29. Ulrich Wilckens, *Die Missionsreden der Apostelgeschichte* (Neukirchen-Vluyn: Neukirchener Verlag, 1961), pp. 152 ff.

future Messiah appointed by God, now waiting in heaven
until that eschatological event when God will send him
to introduce the day of salvation. Significantly, the text
says nothing about the exaltation of Jesus in this period
of waiting. It treats the fact of Jesus' being received into
heaven more in the character of an Old Testament translation or removal story rather than in the triumphant power-
and-glory-bestowing fashion of the exaltation tradition (cf.
Phil. 2:9 ff.).[30] In this connection Hahn interprets Acts
1:9–11 to reflect another formulation of the same tradition.

Like Conzelmann,[31] Hahn interprets Mark 2:18 ff. to be
a reference to the absence of Jesus from his community.
"The statement ὅταν ἀπαρθῇ ἀπ' αὐτῶν ὁ νυμφίος ['when the
bridegroom is taken away from them'] in any case desig-
nates, without prejudice to the use of a metaphor, the time
of the withdrawal of Jesus to heaven. . . ."[32] Hahn contends
that Mark 2:19b and 20, as well as Matthew 25:1 ff., could
only have originated in a community devoid of any knowledge of the exaltation.[33]

Again, and somewhat similar to Conzelmann, Hahn finds
Mark 13 to be "an early Palestinian tradition still relatively
intact."[34] For this chapter, Hahn declares, describes a situation in the early church when the community found itself
still living in the presalvation interim of hardship and
suffering, unaware of "a present activity of Jesus rooted in
the thought of His exaltation. As a 'substitute' the gift of
the Holy Spirit had been given it, but this too was a sign
and token of the ultimate aeon: only later was the Spirit
brought into connection with the heavenly work of Jesus."
In such a situation, Hahn points out, every blasphemy

30. Hahn, *Titles,* pp. 164 ff.; cf. also Fuller, *Foundations,* pp. 159, 184.

31. Hans Conzelmann, "Geschichte und Eschaton nach MK 13," ZNW
50 (1959): 210 ff.

32. Hahn, *Titles,* p. 133.

33. Ibid., p. 92.

34. Ibid., p. 125; cf. Conzelmann, "Geschichte," pp. 210–21.

could be forgiven except the blasphemy against the Holy Spirit (thus Mark 3:28–29).[35]

Already we have examined Hahn's view of Mark 14: 61–62. But a restatement of that view in the present discussion is not inappropriate. Hahn is struck by the fact that Mark 14:61–62 establishes an eschatological setting for the actualization of Psalms 110:1 which is unique to the entire New Testament. This compels him to conclude that this particular passage is the oldest statement we have of the primitive community's belief in Jesus' future messiahship. The linking of Daniel 7:13 to Psalms 110:1 by the earliest community fixes Jesus' enthronement in the parousia-event.[36]

The striking factor in Hahn's reconstruction of this Palestinian tradition from hints in various New Testament passages is that most of the passages which he draws upon come from Mark. That so many of these passages crop up in Mark is neither a coincidence nor an accident. They are there in Mark because the evangelist intentionally drew upon them to support his own christological-eschatological position!

Everything thus far in our discussion points to the fact that Mark still held the early church view that Jesus' enthronement and reunion with his elect occurred only in the "end-time" event called the parousia. Such a view is supported by Mark 2:18 ff. It is underscored in Mark 13:9–13, where the church is characterized as living in a period of suffering without the presence of Jesus, still longing for salvation, and comforted only by the gift of the Holy Spirit. It is supported in Mark 13:6 and 13:21–23, where Mark warns his community against being deceived into believing that Jesus will reappear in the interim of world history. It is verified in 13:24–27 in the actual description of the enthronement of Jesus and his reunion with

---

35. Hahn, *Titles*, pp. 98, 125. See also Robin Scroggs, "The Exaltation of the Spirit by Some Early Christians," *JBL* 84 (1965): 359–73.

36. Hahn, *Titles*, p. 130.

the elect in the final eschatological event. It is substantiated in the importuning of the early community to wait with faith for the return of their absent Lord (Mark 13:28–37), in Jesus' announcement to his disciples that he will not eat again until he does so in the kingdom itself, and in his announcement to the high priest that he will be seen enthroned in the final eschatological event. It is verified by the fact that Mark uses a translation story, consonant with this particular christology, instead of appearance narratives to attest the actuality of the resurrection. It is supported in a negative fashion in that there are no positive and overt attestations in Mark that Jesus' exaltation is understood to be a fait accompli.

What may yet be puzzling to the present reader is how Mark, who is universally believed to have written toward the end of the seventh decade and not later than the early part of the eighth decade A.D., could still hold to such a primitive christological point of view. Evidence (at least Paul) would point to the fact that by Mark's time the church had already shifted its thinking and decided that Jesus had in fact been exalted at his resurrection and was present in some real way with his church. It is a contradiction not expected or easily explained. It makes Mark anachronistic and anomalistic. But despite the strain on credibility, the evidence clearly supports this view.

It may be, however, that Mark is not so unusual in his position if we can place much stock in the Ethiopic text to the Apocalypse of Peter. In this particular apocalypse, written sometime in the early part of the second century and having great similarities to the Markan apocalypse, the last eschatological event is described in a schematic fashion analogous to what has been interpreted for Mark and in somewhat more explicit fashion. Several quotes from the apocalypse makes the point. In a stage setting like that of the Mark 13 apocalypse, Jesus addresses his disciples:

> Take heed that men deceive you not and that ye do not become doubters and serve other gods. Many will come in my

name saying, "I am the Christ." Believe them not and draw not near unto them. For the coming of the Son of God will not be manifest, but like lightning which shineth from east to west, so shall I *come on the clouds of heaven with a great host in my glory;* with my cross going before my face will I come in my glory, shining seven times as bright as the sun will I come in my glory, with all my saints, my angels, *when my Father will place a crown upon my head,* that I may judge the living and the dead and recompense every man according to his work.[37]

Later in the apocalypse we read again:

All will see how *I come upon an eternal shining cloud, and the angels of God who will sit with me on the throne of my glory at the right hand of my heavenly Father. He will set a crown upon my head.* As soon as the nations see it, they will weep, each nation for itself. And he shall command them to go into the river of fire, while the deeds of each individual one of them stand before them. [Recompense shall be given] to each according to his work. As for *the elect who have done good, they will come to me and will not see* death by devouring fire.[38]

The similarities between this apocalypse and what has been conjectured as the Markan position are obvious. Jesus warns his disciples against being deceived into thinking that he is present among them. He will not reappear except in the final cosmic-supernatural event of the eschaton. In that event he will be exalted in glory and installed by God (by crowning) with power and authority. In support of our exegesis of 13:26, the appearance of Jesus is not a descent but an ascent. He does not come to the elect. They come to him!

Mark's couching of the transfiguration story in the context of the parousia was not unintentional. His placing of the resurrection-exaltation story of his opponents in that context served to correct his opponents' christology in favor of his own. The time of Jesus' exaltation is not Easter but the parousia.

37. Edgar Hennecke, *New Testament Apocrypha,* vol. 2, *Writings Relating to the Apostles; Apocalypses and Related Subjects,* ed. Wilhelm Schnee-melcher; Eng. trans. ed. R. McL. Wilson, 2 vols. (Philadelphia: West-minster Press, 1965), p. 668. The italics are mine.

38. Text taken from Hennecke, *New Testament Apocrypha* 2:671–72. Italics are mine.

VI

The Esoteric Kerygma of Mark's Opponents

In his book *Das Messiasgeheimnis in den Evangelium,* Wrede set out to find a theological gestalt that would explain four pervasive motifs in the Markan narrative: Jesus' silencing of the confessions of demons (1:23 ff., 34; 3:11–12; 5:6–7; 9:20), Jesus' command to those healed to seal their lips with regard to their healing (1:44; 5:43; 7:36; 8:26), Jesus' secret instruction to his disciples (4:10–20, 34; 7:14–23; 8:30–31; 9:28 ff., 31; 10:32–34; 13:3 ff.), and the disciples' failure to understand Jesus (4:13, 40–41; 6:50–52; 7:18; 8:16–21; 9:5–6, 19; 10:24; 14:37–41). Guided by 9:9 as the hermeneutical key, Wrede found that these motifs were the constitutive elements of an early Christian apologetic, programmatically applied by Mark, which sought to explain, by way of a messianic secret, why Jesus' messianic nature remained unrecognized until the resurrection.[1] The influence of Wrede upon Markan interpretation has been staggering. Most explanations of the Gospel now take for granted his basic insight.[2]

Wrede's influence on Markan scholarship notwithstanding, a number of conclusions arising from our study raise serious questions about the accuracy of his position and the legitimacy of viewing the messianic secret as the hermeneutical theologumenon of the Gospel.[3] First, the investigation has shown that the disciples' persistent lack of under-

1. William Wrede, *Das Messiasgeheimnis in den Evangelium,* 3d ed. (Göttingen: Vandenhoeck and Ruprecht, 1963), pp. 1–114, particularly pp. 66–69 on Mark 9:9.

2. See David E. Aune, "The Problem of the Messianic Secret," *Nov Test* 11 (1969): 1–31, for a recent survey of the influence of Wrede's position.

3. Hans Conzelmann, "Present and Future in the Synoptic Tradition," trans. Jack Wilson, *JTC* 5 (1968): 43, contends that the "secrecy theory is the hermeneutical presupposition of the genre, 'gospel.'"

standing in the drama does not serve as a component factor in a messianic secret motif. Rather, it is a polemical element in the evangelist's vendetta against the disciples. Second, our investigation has shown that Jesus' messianic identity is not always concealed during the public ministry. It is true that some messianic titles are suppressed (e.g. 1:24–25; 3:11–12; 8:29–30), but Jesus in straightforward fashion affirms and openly proclaims his identity as the Son of man (2:10, 28; 8:31–32; 14:62). Third, the investigation of Mark's use of his opponents' resurrection story (9:2–8) has shown that Mark closes the story with the comment, "He charged them to tell no one what they had seen, until the Son of man should have risen from the dead" (9:9), but not with the purpose of setting forth a hermeneutical principle by which one should recognize that the Gospel is to be interpreted through a messianic secret motif. Mark 9:9 in the evangelist's schema has no more profound function than to serve as an explanatory remark to the reader, explicating why the resurrection story of the evangelist's opponents could not have been a bona fide resurrection experience.

If the persistent failure of the disciples to understand Jesus is not part of a messianic secret, if Jesus does publicly acknowledge his messianic identity before Easter, if 9:9 no longer retains central importance in interpreting the Markan secrecy motif, then how are we to understand the secrecy theme which does permeate the Gospel, even to its final verse (16:8b)? The logical place to seek an answer to that question is in the passage where the clearest statement of a secrecy theme can be found: 4:11–12.

The Tradition behind Mark 4:1–34 and the So-called Markan Parable Theory

The focal point for the interpretation of Mark 4 since Wrede has centered around 4:11–12 and 4:34.[4] Most

---

4. See particularly Willi Marxsen, "Redaktionsgeschichtliche Erklärung der sogenannten Parabeltheorie des Markus," *ZTK* 52 (1955): 255–71; G. H. Boobyer, "The Redaction of Mark iv. 1–34," *NTS* 8 (1961): 59–77;

exegetes have argued that Mark, by impregnating his material with 4:11–12 and 4:34, has indelibly imprinted on the parable chapter and the whole Gospel his theory that Jesus' parables, and teachings generally, were to remain purposely incomprehensible to all except the disciples. The disciples alone were chosen to be the recipients of their secret meaning. While this assessment of Markan redaction and purpose has received wide support, it nevertheless produces some critical hermeneutical problems.

First, if 4:34, asserting that Jesus taught only in parables, is Markan redaction, then Mark must have either been a very careless, inconsistent writer or very feebleminded thinker. For even a cursory reading of the Gospel shows that Jesus did not teach *only* in parables. Second, if 4:34 and 4:11–12 are labeled as Markan redactional activity in which the evangelist is claiming that Jesus' teachings are always obscure to outsiders and understood alone by the disciples—and then only after secret instruction—Mark again betrays his literary and intellectual ineptitude. For the Syrophoenician woman (7:27 ff.), the rich young man (10:17–22), the scribes (12:28–34), and the Pharisees (12:1–12), to name just a few, do understand Jesus.

Third, contrary to what one would expect from the disciples as exclusive recipients of Jesus' secret instruction (4:11–12, 34), of all participants in this Markan christological drama, they are the most obtuse. These confidants of Jesus continually fail to understand his teaching and at least twice are accused of hardness of heart (6:52; 8:17), the type of response to Jesus' teachings one would expect from outsiders (4:11–12, cf. 3:5, 10:5), not the disciples.[5]

J. Gnilka, *Die Verstockung Israels* (Munich: Kösel, 1961), pp. 25 ff., 62–82; E. Linnemann, *Jesus of the Parables*, trans. J. Sturdy (New York: Harper & Row, 1966), pp. 118–80; Eduard Schweizer, *The Good News According to Mark*, trans. D. H. Madvig (Richmond, Va.: John Knox Press, 1970), pp. 88 ff.; Quentin Quesnell, *The Mind of Mark*, Analecta Biblica, no. 38 (Rome: Pontifical Biblical Institute, 1969), pp. 72–88.

5. In contradiction to the motif of 4:11–12 the Pharisees do understand Jesus' parable in Mark 12:1 ff. That this is so is suggested by the use of γινώσκειν (to know) in 12:12. γινώσκειν is often employed by Mark as a verb of recognition and penetrating insight (cf. 4:13; 8:17; 13:28, 29; 15:10).

Fourth, the insertion of 4:21–25 by Mark[6] flies in the face of the supposed addition of 4:11–12 and 34. In opposition to the secrecy motif of 4:11–12, 34, which contends that the meaning of Jesus' teachings is to remain hidden to all but to the select few to whom it is guardedly revealed, the theme of 4:21–25 depicts just the reverse. The sayings of the exposed lamplight and the shared measure place the emphasis on a revelation motif that sets no limits on the scope of the revelation or its recipients. These blatant incongruities raise serious questions about the adequacy of the traditional interpretation of Mark 4 and of its place and purpose in the Gospel as a whole.

Eduard Schweizer has proposed a compelling solution to this hermeneutical problem. In a refreshing, new insight Schweizer contends that 4:11–12 already belonged to the tradition which included the parable of the sower and its interpretation. He finds 4:11–12 to be terminologically and theologically alien to Mark. Terminologically, the word that leaps out at us in 4:11 is the word μυστήριον (secret). Strangely, though one is conscious of a secrecy motif in the Gospel, the term μυστήριον (secret, mystery) occurs only in this one instance. This in itself might not be so extraordinary if it were not for the theological connotations usually associated with this term in late Jewish apocalypticism, particularly at Qumran. According to a dominant theme in Jewish apocalyptic thought, God reveals his mystery or mysteries to the elect but conceals them from the world, which remains helplessly lost in its own blindness. A Christian adaptation of this theme lies unmistakably behind 1 Corinthians 2:6 ff., Romans 16:25 ff., Colossians 1:25–26, 2:2–3, Ephesians 3:1 ff., 1 Timothy 3:16. In the Christian formulation of the mystery, revealed to the elect but hidden from the world, Christ himself is that mystery, the one who died but now reigns triumphantly.[7]

6. See Joachim Jeremias, *The Parables of Jesus*, trans. S. H. Hooke, rev. ed. (New York: Charles Scribner's Sons, 1963), pp. 14, 91; Gnilka, *Die Verstockung*, pp. 61–62.
7. Eduard Schweizer, "Zur Frage des Messiasgeheimnisses bei Markus," *ZNW* 56 (1965): 1–2. For important Qumran passages see 1QS 11:3–4,

Theologically, Schweizer argues that the position advocated by 4:11–12 is really incompatible with the theological
thrust of the rest of Mark's Gospel. According to the
secret, the elect—in Mark's case, the disciples—are supposed
to both fully comprehend and act as guardians of the
sacred mystery. For the world—in Mark's case, "the outsiders"—the secret is incomprehensible. They remain forever blind to the secret's meaning (cf. John 12:40; Acts
28:26–27). The problem, Schweizer notes, is that this particular pattern fails to hold true for the Gospel. The disciples remain blind to the mystery. No sooner are we told
that the disciples are recipients of special understanding
than we are told that their facility for understanding is
limited (4:13b). On the basis of this inconsistency
Schweizer contends that 4:11–12 and 4:13b could not have
come from the same writer.

Mark 4:11–12, Schweizer declares, is more akin to the
theological perspective of 4:14–20. It is in this passage
that we find the esoteric, allegorical interests associated with
Jewish apocalyptic thought that perceives the elect to be
custodians of enigmatic teaching, the meaning of which is
possessed alone by them. Schweizer concludes that 4:11–12
was added to the parable of the sower and its interpretation before it reached Mark's hand.[8]

If we accept Schweizer's theory about 4:11–12, then the
inconsistency attributed to Mark can no longer be charged
solely to Mark's own hand but to a conflict between
Markan theology and his source. That is, the dissonance
between the pattern of hiddenness and revelation proclaimed in 4:11–12 and that which is actualized in the rest
of the Gospel can be accounted for by the fact that 4:11–12

18–19; 1QH 7:26–27; 10:2–3; 11:3–4, 10; 12:11–13; 1QpHab 7:25. See
also Günther Bornkamm, "μυστήριον," *TDNT* 4:815–16, for a discussion
on the place of μυστήριον (secret, mystery) in Jewish apocalypticism.
Schweizer is indebted to Erik Sjöberg, *Der verborgene Menschensohn in
den Evangelien* (Lund, Sweden: C. W. K. Gleerup, 1955), pp. 150 ff.,
for seeing the relationship of the secrecy motif of Mark 4:11–12 to the
secrecy motif of Jewish apocalypticism.

8. Schweizer, "Zur Frage," pp. 4–7.

belonged to Mark's source. If 4:11–12 belonged to Mark's source, then what about 4:34, which supports the hermeneutical principle articulated in 4:11–12?

Against the traditional interpretation, Joachim Gnilka presents formidable evidence for the non-Markan origin of 4:34, namely, the singular occurrence in Mark of the words χωρίς (without) and ἐπιλύειν (to reveal), the designation τοῖς ἰδίοις μαθηταῖς (his own disciples), and the rather unusual usage of the connective particle δέ in successive clauses by an author who has such a strong proclivity for καί. Furthermore, the presence and thrust of ἐπιλύειν in v. 34 place the tenor of the verse in harmony with the pre-Markan tradition that had already moved in the direction of interpreting parables allegorically. The substantive ἐπίλυσις and verb ἐπιλύειν, as Gnilka shows, are frequently found in the literature of antiquity with reference to the interpretation of riddles, dreams, and prophecies. In the Shepherd of Hermas ἐπιλύειν and ἐπίλυσις are used similarly to the way ἐπιλύειν is employed in Mark 4:34, in association with the allegorical interpretation of parables.[9]

Such non-Markan linguistic characteristics, along with the allegorical and esoteric thrust of ἐπιλύειν, argue strongly for the claim that v. 34 is not a Markan creation but rather belongs to the pre-Markan material. It fits well with the hermeneutical style and interest of the community that interpreted the parable of the sower allegorically. Moreover, to argue that v. 34 is Markan redaction—that is, to argue that Mark's theory is that Jesus taught only in parables—raises the formidable problem of explaining why Mark introduces so much material that patently and devastatingly runs counter to this theory. Just in terms of the quantity of material involved it is far easier to explain the thematic opposition between a singular verse and numerous passages by suggesting that that one verse merely represents a minor

9. Gnilka, *Die Verstockung*, pp. 59 ff. Cf. The Shepherd of Hermas 5,3,1–2; 5,4,2–3; 5,5,1; 5,6,8; 5,7,1; 8,11,1; 9,10,5; 9,11,9; 9,13,9; 9,16,7. Schweizer, *The Good News*, p. 59, argues the same for 34b.

case of an editorial oversight. By the same logic, the teaching motif—hidden to the masses, revealed exclusively to the disciples—of v. 34 is easier explained as belonging to a pre-Markan tradition. This judgment appears particularly sound in view of the overwhelming evidence elsewhere in Mark that Jesus does not teach with the view of making his message obscure to the masses and in view of the fact that the only people to whom Jesus' message appears obscure and incomprehensible is the disciples.

The concept of the esoteric meaning of parables, the so-called messianic secret, was already a part of the tradition which Mark received. The positions customarily attributed to Mark and his received material respectively are really just the reverse. Mark's received material argues for hidden, exclusive, esoteric teaching. Mark argues for openness, revelation on a nonexclusive basis! The Markan insertions of 4:21–25, the exposed lamplight and the shared measure, clearly pinpoint what Mark intends to be self-evident: the teachings of Jesus are quite lucid, not at all intended to be veiled in secrecy, and are available to all.

If this be the case, then why did Mark use material that sets itself in such diametric opposition to his own point of view? A clue to the answer to this question is uncovered when one recognizes that the theological slant of 4:11–12, 14–20, 34 coincides well with *theios-aner* theology.

The theological compatibility of these passages with the *theios-aner* kerygma can be shown on several counts.

First, the focus on a secret and exclusive kerygma, concealed from all except those who belong to the narrow circle of the elect (4:11–12, 33–34) is in complete harmony with the *theios-aner* attitude. Second, the recourse to allegorical interpretation, such as is found in 4:14–20, in order to extrapolate from the literal text of scripture the sacred mysteries is a hermeneutical technique employed by those of the *theios-aner* persuasion.

An excellent example of this *theios-aner* mind-set is posed by the Corinthian *theioi andres* (2 Cor. 2:14–7:4; 10–13).

In contrast to Paul, the *theioi andres* at Corinth had great confidence and pride in the fact that they possessed a secret gospel whose meaning was hidden from all but themselves. Of paramount importance to their kerygmatic position was their ability to extract from Old Testament texts spiritual meaning and power which they viewed as absolutely essential to Christian edification and spiritual perfection. But this spiritual power so essential to the Christian life was hidden from the ordinary eye by the literal meaning of the text. Only through the correct allegorical interpretation guided by the Spirit (which the opponents claimed they possessed) could one uncover from the literal text the spiritual power beneath. When this was accomplished these *theioi andres* claimed that one was thrust into an encounter with God and the mystery of his message. These Corinthian heretics looked upon this strong emphasis upon the secret character of their preaching not as an obstacle but as a boon to drawing converts to them.[10]

Another kinship with the theological perspective of 4:11–12 and the *theios-aner* position can be found in the secrecy motif which Johannes Schreiber contends lies at the heart of a *theios-aner* crucifixion tradition in Mark. Through critical analysis, Schreiber has been able to separate out the component parts of the Markan crucifixion narrative (15:20b–41) before they were woven together by the evangelist. What Schreiber has uncovered are two crucifixion traditions. One, the earlier of the two, is represented by 15:20b, 22, 24, 27. At the heart of that narrative is a theological apologetic which draws upon, at least by allusion, the Old Testament texts of Psalms 22:18 (Mark 15:24) and Isaiah 53:12 (Mark 15:27) to prove that Jesus was an innocent, righteous one of God, put to death by his enemies.

The second crucifixion tradition, found in Mark 15:25, 26,

10. See Dieter Georgi, *Die Gegner des Paulus im 2. Korintherbrief* (Neukirchen-Vluyn: Neukirchener Verlag, 1964), pp. 175–82 and particularly 265–82.

29a, 32c, 33, 34a, 37, 38, Schreiber claims, is a narrative describing the death of Jesus, framed in the language and themes of Old Testament Jewish-apocalyptic interests. The basic theme is that the godless, who at present are in control of the earth, crucify the Messiah. That is why darkness covers the earth (v. 33). As in the beginning, before creation, darkness and chaos reign (Gen. 1:2). In the course of the crucifixion these godless ones mock the Messiah (v. 29a) and revile him (v. 32c). In so doing they expose themselves to be blind sinners.

The triumphant moment in the narrative comes when Jesus cries out from the cross (vv. 34a, 37). Like the voice of God in Genesis 1:3, which cries out bringing order out of chaos, ending the rule of darkness and establishing the rule of light, Jesus' cry is both a judgment of and a triumph over the rule of darkness. The effect of this cry of triumph is that the old world order, symbolized by the temple veil, is destroyed (v. 38), Jesus is revealed as exalted, and the pious of God are introduced to the new world of light.

Running through the narrative, Schreiber argues, is a secrecy motif which exhibits striking similarity to the hidden-redeemer motif of 1 Corinthians 2:8 and Philippians 2:6 ff. The enemies of the redeemer are blinded to the fact that they crucify the redeemer, a fact that is hidden from them until his death-exaltation. The fact that the second crucifixion narrative casts the preaching of the cross in the stylized format of Hellenistic epiphany stories, Schreiber argues, attests to its creation by a Hellenistic-Jewish community which had fallen under the influence of Hellenistic religiosity of the *theios-aner* perspective.[11] The

11. Johannes Schreiber, *Theologie des Vertrauens* (Hamburg: Furche-Verlag H. Rennebach K. G., 1967), pp. 24–40; 66–82. This historicizing of the kerygma, Schreiber says, is a radical departure from that which one finds in Palestinian Jewish Christianity and other sectors of Hellenistic Jewish Christianity. The Palestinian church never made use of Hellenistic-style epiphany stories. The Pauline circle did not narrate events in Jesus' life as pictorial preaching of a past event which at the same time encompasses the future (e.g., the reference to the destruction of the temple: Mark 15:38). See *Theologie*, pp. 70 ff.

kinship between this *theios-aner* crucifixion narrative and its secrecy motif and the secrecy motif of 4:11–12 is unmistakable. This is particularly evident when one bears in mind Schweizer's conclusion that the theological position proclaimed in 4:11–12 is best traced back to the Christian adaptation (1 Cor. 2:6 ff.) of the secrecy motif of Jewish apocalypticism.[12]

Since Mark 4:11–12, 14–20, 34 exhibit a theological perspective consonant with *theios-aner* theology, one has good reason to conclude that these passages belonged to Mark's *theios-aner* opponents. To push the matter further: it is my judgment that the parable of the sower (4:3–9) and its interpretation (4:14–20), plus the parables of the growing seed (4:26–29) and the mustard seed (4:30–32) and the concluding statement to this cluster of parables (4:33–34)[13] belonged to Mark's opponents. In 4:11–12 Mark provides us with the hermeneutical rationale and proof text for their view on parabolic instruction, as well as for their entire kerygmatic position. It was the superimposing of this hermeneutical perspective upon the parables in Mark 4 that caused Jeremias to detect in the chapter a change in the original meaning of the word *parable* from "parable" to "riddle."[14]

It hardly needs to be said that Mark was vehemently opposed to this *theios-aner* position (see, e.g., 4:21–25). To him it was an aberrant and insidious bastardization of the faith. But he could not ignore its impressive claims or dismiss it out of hand. Apparently too many in Mark's

---

12. According to Schreiber, *Theologie*, p. 77, in compiling his Gospel Mark borrowed the secrecy motif of the hidden redeemer from the second crucifixion narrative, and, under the influence of the crucified-secret-redeemer theme of Philippians 2:6 ff. and 1 Corinthians 2:8, superimposed a messianic secret upon the other epiphany stories, making it the hermeneutical principle of his Gospel.

13. Quesnell, *Mark*, pp. 84 ff., demonstrates that vv. 33 ff. are a "reaffirmation" of 4:11–12. Vincent Taylor, *The Mind of Mark*, (London: Macmillan and Co., 1959), p. 271, and Gnilka, *Die Verstockung*, pp. 59–60 argue that vv. 33 and 34 belonged to Mark's source. Gnilka's persuasive argument on verse 34 has already been cited above.

14. Jeremias, *Parables*, pp. 16 ff.

community had been won over by the appeal of a secret
gospel.

Consequently Mark had to mount a persuasive polemic
against it. He saw that the most convincing way to discredit the claims of a secret gospel would be to take its
basic components (its rationale, terminology, secrecy motif,
and so on) and either expose them as absurd or eviscerate
them by turning them into weapons in the service of his
own position, or both. His schema for doing this took
several different directions. First, he exposed the position
of his opponents as ludicrous by demonstrating the absurdity
of its hermeneutical principle as it was actualized in the
response of the Twelve and outsiders to Jesus. We have
already observed at length in chapter 1 how Mark stages
this particular aspect of his polemic. Only a brief recapitu-
lation is needed for the sake of the current argument. In
4:11–12 Mark has Jesus proclaim to the disciples that they
hold a favored status. To them will be revealed the mystery
of the kingdom. But to everyone outside, Jesus' message
will be enigmatic. Outsiders will see but not perceive, hear
but not understand. In practice, as we have noted on
several occasions, just the reverse occurs. Outsiders do seem
to perceive and understand things about Jesus. The disciples, though privy to the so-called mystery, are found
completely wanting in comprehension. They are the ones
who see but don't perceive and hear but don't understand
(see particularly 4:13; 6:51–52; 7:14–19; 8:17–21; 9:32).

I have implicitly suggested, if not explicitly stated, on
various occasions in the course of this book that the disciples
serve as surrogates of the Markan opponents. This fact
must be clearly enunciated at this point. In all likelihood
the *theioi andres* in Mark's community based their position
on a tradition that they contended went back to the disciples
themselves.[15] Recognition of this surrogate relationship be-

15. An analogue to this practice can be found in the Signs Source of
John, where the *theioi-andres* propagators of that document drew upon
the authority of the disciples to authenticate their claims (John 20:30).
See above, pp. 58–59.

tween the disciples and the *theioi andres* in Mark's community facilitates our understanding of the scope of Mark's
purpose in demonstrating that the proclamation of 4:
11–12[16] is actualized in reverse. Mark's message is that the
hermeneutical principle of his opponents is absurd; one
would discover the meaning of the Gospel better from outsiders than from his opponents or their surrogates.[17]

16. Marxsen, "Parabeltheorie," pp. 263 ff. argues that the linking of the
Twelve with οἱ περὶ αὐτόν to create the expression "those about him with
the Twelve" is Mark's attempt to contemporize the scene and link the
community with the tradition that lies behind Mark 4. I believe that
the reference to "those . . . with the Twelve" is Mark's cue to the
reader that he is pointing to those people in the community who are to
be identified with the tradition of the Twelve and for whom the Twelve
serve as surrogates in the Gospel.

17. Before concluding our discussion of 4:11–12 we must address ourselves to an important point by Jeremias which argues against Schweizer's
conclusion that Mark 4:11–12 was set in its present context before Mark.
In his exegesis of Mark 4 Jeremias has convincingly argued that καὶ
ἔλεγεν (and he said) represents a connectional link for material used
by a pre-Markan editor and that καὶ ἔλεγεν αὐτοῖς (and he said to them)
represents a connectional link used by Mark in his own redaction (Jeremias,
Parables, p. 14). Following Jeremias, one would have to argue that
Schweizer is wrong. Actually, both Schweizer and Jeremias are correct.
Schweizer is obviously correct when assigning 4:11–12 to the pre-Markan
tradition which included the parable of the sower and its interpretation.
For 4:11–12 unmistakably runs counter to the theological thrust of Mark's
Gospel. But Jeremias is also right in claiming that Mark added 4:11–12
at 4:10.
   Mark 4:11–12 was a part of the Markan opponents' tradition which
included the parable of the sower and its interpretation. But in that
tradition the secrecy declaration (4:11–12) did not appear between the
parable and the interpretation. It is possible that it could have followed
originally upon 4:34, but there is no way to substantiate that, although
there is similarity in the antithetical parallelism of the two passages.
   Mark introduced this hermeneutical principle of his enemies between
the parable and its interpretation to set the stage for the denigration of
the disciples. Prior to this point in the narrative there is only a small
hint (1:35 ff.) that the disciples might not be in full accord with Jesus'
ministry or might in any way not understand him. With 4:13b the full
force of Mark's vendetta against the disciples and his opponents begins.
The key to his schema to undermine the reader's confidence in the disciples
(and through them the evangelist's opponents) lies in Mark's turning the
theologumenon of his enemies against them. Since he found this theologumenon in the parable tradition of his enemies, it would not have
made much sense to introduce the secrecy theory of his enemies outside
the context of parabolic discussion. Thus Mark could not have introduced
it before 4:2.

Second, not only does Mark make his opponents' claim
to a secret gospel ludicrous by showing how absurd their
hermeneutical principle is, but he also eviscerates the secret
gospel by adopting its terminology in the service of his own
suffering-christology apologetic. Once one recognizes that
4:14–20 belongs in the service of an allegorical apologetic
of Mark's *theios-aner* opponents, a new and profound meaning of the absolute rendering of the term ὁ λόγος (the word)
comes to the fore. The word λόγος occurs fifteen times in
the singular, absolute, unqualified usage in the Gospel.
Eight of these occurrences are to be found in 4:14–20. The

Likewise, if he was to undercut his opponents' kerygmatic position with
the full devastating force required he could not have introduced the
secrecy motif after 4:14. By the nature of his attack upon the disciples
and the opponents' tradition they represent, he had to show at the outset
that the disciples were incapable of fathoming the meaning of Jesus' parabolic instruction. This accounts for the insertion of the remark at 4:13
which indicates that the disciples did not understand the parable of the
sower. To have inserted the secrecy motif (4:11–12) after 4:13 would
not have produced as telling an indictment of the disciples as is produced
by its present location before reference to the disciples' lack of comprehension. By the resulting juxtaposition of the clashing viewpoints of 4:
11–12 and 4:13, the strident dissonance between the disciples' so-called
favored position and the actual nature of the disciples' performance is
vividly dramatized.

18. In terms of vocabulary and theological perspective, 4:33 fits the position advocated in 4:11–12 and 34 better than Mark's own position. The
connotation of the word παραβολή (parable) is the same as its connotation in 4:11–12. It means riddle. This particular emphasis on Jesus'
teaching as riddles—in other words, intentionally hidden—is not consonant
with Mark's theological perspective of Jesus' teaching. Another word
which exhibits pre-Markan character in this verse is λαλεῖν (to speak
or proclaim). While this word is used on occasion by Mark in passages
fashioned with his own pen (e.g., 8:32; 13:11; 14:9), the word occurs
for the most part in passages that do not show clear Markan fingerprints
(e.g., 2:7; 4:34; 5:35, 36; 6:50; 7:35, 37; 14:31, 43). λαλεῖν does not
appear to be a word peculiar to Markan redaction but rather appears to
be derived from his tradition. This judgment is supported further by a
reflection upon the way in which Mark cites Jesus' teaching. Mark usually
depicts the teaching or preaching activity in redactional passages with
the words διδάσκειν (to teach), διδαχή (teaching), κηρύσσειν (to preach)
(see Eduard Schweizer, "Anmerkungen zur Theologie des Markus,"
Neotestamentica et Patristica, ed. W. C. van Unnik [Leiden: E. J. Brill,
1962], pp. 37–38; idem, "Mark's Contribution to the Quest of the Historical
Jesus," *NTS* 10 [1964]: 422–23). Jeremias argues for the pre-Markan
origin of 4:33 solely on the basis of the presence of the absolute usage of
ὁ λόγος (Jeremias, *Parables,* p. 14).

seven other instances are located in 1:45; 2:2; 4:33; 5:36; 8:32; 9:10; 10:22. Eleven usages of this particular form of λόγος are clearly found in pre-Markan tradition (4:14, 15, 16, 17, 18, 19, 20, 33;[18] 5:36; 10:22).[19]

What is the import of this singular absolute, unqualified usage of ὁ λόγος for the Markan community? Ulrich Luz asserts that ὁ λόγος is a thoroughly positive expression which Mark borrowed from the tradition before him and which, as one complete term, symbolically represents the summation of Christian preaching. Johannes Schreiber and T. A. Burkill interpret ὁ λόγος to be an expression tantamount to the word *gospel* in Mark. In fact Schreiber categorizes the term as the gospel of the passion and enthronization of Jesus for the Gentiles.[20] In my opinion ὁ λόγος is Mark's opponents' term for gospel, their secret gospel.

Mark appropriates his enemies' term for gospel and deftly turns it to the defense of his own apologetic and to an assault on his enemies' kerygma. The most significant instance of this is to be found in 8:32, particularly when one recalls that this verse is lodged in the midst of the sharp conflict between Jesus and Peter over the character of authentic christology.

Jesus drops a bombshell upon Peter and his *theios-aner* interests in 8:31 by explicating for the first time the kerygma of suffering christology. As soon as this is declared by Jesus, Mark follows with a ringing commentary: καὶ παρρησίᾳ τὸν λόγον ἐλάλει (and he proclaimed *the word openly*). In this quick stroke Mark strikes at the heart of his opponents' theology. By adopting their term for gospel

19. Two instances in which this usage of ὁ λόγος is found in Markan redaction are 8:32 and 9:10. The term also occurs in 1:45 and 2:2, passages customarily identified as showing evidence of Markan redaction. In view of the specialized use of ὁ λόγος in his opponents' tradition (see below), it is not impossible that the occurrence of ὁ λόγος in 1:45 and 2:2 may have been lodged in the introduction (2:2) and the conclusion (1:45) of the two stories Mark received and subsequently edited.

20. Cf. Ulrich Luz, "Das Geheimnismotiv und die Markanische Christologie," *ZNW* 56 (1965): 16; Schreiber, *Theologie*, pp. 110–11; T. A. Burkill, *Mysterious Revelation* (Ithaca, N. Y.: Cornell University Press, 1963), p. 172. Cf. also Jeremias, *Parables*, p. 77.

to underscore the suffering christology of Jesus, he empties
it of its *theios-aner* meaning and suggests that the real content of ὁ λόγος, the gospel the enemies claim to have special
possession of, is not the power christology they claim but
the suffering christology that Jesus unfolds to Peter. Moreover, by stating that he spoke *the word* παρρησίᾳ (openly),
Mark, in opposition to the esoteric claims of his enemies,
stresses the unambiguous, unconcealed character of Jesus'
christological teaching. In the wording of 8:32 the evangelist
may very well have intended to parody his opponents' position in 4:33. Mark 4:33, translated with all the nuances of
the opponents' views, should read: "and in many such
riddles Jesus proclaimed the *gospel.*" In parodied contrast,
8:32 reads, "he proclaimed the *gospel openly* [plainly]."[21]

Mark's use of his opponents' term for gospel in 9:10 is
intended as a mimicry of the *theios-aner* kerygma. Mark
asserts that the disciples *kept to themselves* "the gospel"
about Jesus' future glorification at the parousia (9:10a). Yet
despite the fact that they are the possessors of a secret
gospel, they fail really to understand the heart of the gospel
which has as its content the suffering death and resurrection
of Jesus (8:31 ff.; 9:5 ff., 32). They treat as a riddle that
which is plain; namely, the whole content of Jesus' message
to them, that he is going to suffer and die and be raised.
They may pride themselves on possessing a secret gospel
(ὁ λόγος), but it is an empty, meaningless gospel. For since
it is a gospel that has no understanding of suffering-servant
messiahship, it is then a gospel for which the resurrection
has no meaning (9:10b).

Other significant echoes of this same terminological
polemic in areas of Mark's Gospel where Jesus refers to his
teaching by the opponents' technical term λόγος are found
in the occurrences of λόγος in 8:38; 13:31; and 14:39. Mark

21. Quesnell, *Mark*, pp. 173–74 also notes that the contrast between
4:33–34 and 8:32 was deliberately contrived by Mark. But he erroneously
accounts for it as brought about by Mark's shift in emphasis on the
nature of Jesus' teaching: before 8:31, Jesus' kerygma is intentionally
hidden; after 8:31, it is openly proclaimed.

8:38 follows at the conclusion of the christological conflict between Peter and Jesus and immediately after Jesus has urged the disciples and the crowd present with them to commit themselves to his εὐαγγέλιον (gospel), the path of suffering christology and discipleship. If need be, one is to lose his life for the sake of this εὐαγγέλιον. Such a person will discover salvation. However, should anyone be ashamed of his *words* (τοὺς ἐμοὺς λόγους), the Son of man will be ashamed of him when he comes glorified with the angels. Mark makes a play on words in this verse, using an allusion to the enemies' term for gospel to repudiate them for their rejection of the authentic gospel which Jesus has preached and lived.

Likewise, Mark makes a play on his opponents' technical term for gospel in 14:39. When Jesus prays for the second time that the suffering cup might pass from him (yet accepts God's desire for it) the passage tells us that he went to pray "the same word" (τὸν αὐτὸν λόγον). Again we have a double entendre. Jesus' prayer expressed in the terminology of the opponents' word for gospel has as its content Mark's understanding of gospel.

Finally, in 13:31 Jesus promises that his *words* will not pass away. The echo of the opponents' technical term is heard again. It resonates in this case in the context and by way of the content of the Markan eschatological and christological message. The enemies are thus undone by Mark's use of their own term against them and in support of his own kerygma. The members of Mark's church learn that Jesus recognizes the legitimacy of the opponents' technical term for gospel only when it points to Mark's kerygma.

A third way in which Mark eviscerates his opponents' position is by appropriating their secrecy motif in the service of his polemic against them. He uses a secrecy motif on the one hand to have Jesus impose silence upon *theios-aner* messianic confessions and on the other hand to have Jesus suppress the publicizing of his success as a miracle worker.

Mark has Jesus muzzle demonic confessions not because he wants his messianic identity hidden until Easter (the view of Wrede and others)—not at all. Mark's Jesus does not silence all christological confessions. Mark is quite happy to have Jesus known as the Son of man (2:10, 28; 8:31–32, 38; 14:62). It is the one christological title in the Gospel that is neither rejected nor silenced. It is the one title that Jesus accepts for himself and vigorously proclaims (8:31–32, 38; 9:12, 31; 10:33; 13:26; 14:62). The reasons for this we already know. The suffering Son-of-man christology which Jesus claims is Mark's own christology.

Mark's Jesus silences only the wrong christological confessions. He muzzles those confessions to his christological nature whose connotation or meaning is solely an identification of Jesus as a *theios-aner* Christ. That is the reason for silencing the unclean spirits in 3:11–12 and 5:7. Both of these instances of the confession of Jesus as the Son of God are evoked as a consequence of Jesus' demonstration of his miraculous capacity to exorcise demonic spirits.[22] For the same reason Jesus silences the unclean spirits in 1:25 and 34. They likewise proclaim Jesus to be a *theios-aner* Christ. In fact all unclean spirits in the Markan Gospel know Jesus as a *theios-aner* Christ (3:11). That, in Mark's eyes, is heretical christology. Such confessions must be silenced.

Jesus' refusal to allow the healed to talk of their healing is again a function of a polemic against the *theios-aner* christology. These people are not silenced, as Wrede and others claimed, because Mark is trying to conceal Jesus' messianic status until Easter. Those who are healed are silenced (1:44; 5:43; 7:36; 8:26) because Mark is trying to play down the dramatic character of Jesus' miracle working, lest it mislead his readers into seeing Jesus primarily as a *theios aner*—and thereby unwittingly cause them to

22. So also Schweizer, *The Good News*, p. 358.

succumb to the appeal of the *theios-aner* christology of Mark's opponents.[23]

The only points at which Mark will allow a *theios-aner* title to stand unsilenced is when the title has been properly reinterpreted in terms of Son-of-man christology. At the transfiguration the voice from the clouds attests to the fact that Jesus is God's Son and admonishes the disciples to listen to him (9:7). This admonishment to listen to Jesus is a throwback to Jesus' prediction of the passion in 8:31–32, thereby informing the reader that the voice from heaven understands sonship in terms of a suffering Son of man. A similar christological interpretation of the Son-of-God title can be found in 14:61–62. Jesus is asked by the high priest if he is the Son of the Blessed. Jesus responds affirmatively but defines divine sonship in categories of the

23. It would be wrong to argue that Mark is totally opposed to recognizing that Jesus was a success as a *theios aner*. He must admit this success if for no other reason than for the sake of staging his polemic against his enemies. But it must be unmistakably stated that Mark was utterly opposed to interpreting Jesus' success as a *theios aner* as the clue that enables one to recognize that Jesus is the Messiah. In fact Mark would claim that, on the contrary, one's preoccupation with Jesus' *theios-aner* activity blinds one to the true character of his messiahship. In this regard the violation of Jesus' injunction to silence in 7:36–37 is not at all inconsistent with this interpretation of the purpose behind Jesus' desire to keep his miracle-working feats unknown. Even though the people present at the healing of the deaf-mute refuse to obey the Markan Jesus, Jesus has still made his point. He does not want the focus of people's attention to be on his powers as a miracle worker, lest it blind people to the essential trait in his life-style: his suffering servanthood. Those who, against Jesus' admonition, insist on dwelling on his miracle-working power—such as the people of 7:36–37—are like the disciples: they never see or understand Jesus' true nature.

Likewise, Mark's failure to alter Jesus' injunction to the healed demoniac to spread the news of his cure (5:1–20) can be explained on the basis of the way in which Mark steered his argumentative course between Scylla and Charybdis. Even Mark could not have allowed the negative note of 5:16–17 to dominate the narrative. To superimpose silence on the healed demoniac would have left the narrative with an almost totally negative tone. At the same time, the narrative was important for him in setting up the *theios-aner* position in the first half of the Gospel. Mark probably found the narrative acceptable as it is because of the fact that Jesus refuses the man permission to be a part of his following. Mark could legitimately argue that Jesus' refusal of the man's request is evidence enough that faith in him as a miracle worker does not qualify one to be his follower.

Son-of-man christology.[24] Likewise, the centurion's confession that Jesus is the Son of God is a legitimate confession
because the centurion makes that confession by virtue of
witnessing the living out of Son-of-man christology.[25]

If all these factors usually attributed to the traditional
explanation of the messianic secret are really used in a
polemic against a *theios-aner* christology, then what about
the occasions in the Gospel when Jesus withdraws from
public view and wishes to be alone with his disciples? For
example, when Jesus retires into a house, or retreats to a
desert, or climbs into a boat, or ascends a mountain, are
not these clear instances of the Markan Jesus' desire to
choose secrecy and thus, as Wrede and others have interpreted it, keep his messiahship hidden?

The boat motif, as Keck has convincingly shown,[26] is a
motif which belonged to a collection of stories from a
theios-aner tradition. It is my opinion that this collection
of boat stories came from the repertoire of Mark's opponents.
The boat motif has no particular theological import for
the evangelist. With respect to Mark's use of a desert motif,
the desert is a place for seeking solace in the Gospel (1:35;
6:31–32), a place of temptation (1:12–13), and a place
of public revelation (1:3–4, 45; 6:35 ff.). Jesus' retreat to
the desert places does not support the conventional understanding of the secrecy motif.

24. So also Norman Perrin, "The Christology of Mark: A Study in
Methodology" (paper presented at the Seminar on Christology of the
New Testament at the Annual Meeting of the Studiorum Novi Testamenti
Societas, New Castle upon Tyne, England, August 1970; and idem,
"Towards an Interpretation of the Gospel of Mark," unpublished paper).

25. At first it might appear that 1:11 is an exception to Mark's practice
of imposing silence on the use of the Son-of-God title unless it is clearly
interpreted by Son-of-man christology. However, while the title stands
without immediate correction, the voice of God in 9:7 unmistakably indicates what God means when he uses this title. With regard to 1:1, the
occurrence of the title *Son of God* is strongly contested by good manuscript evidence. Even if it is authentic, there can be little doubt in the
reader's mind what christological connotation the title had for Mark.

26. Leander Keck, "Mark 3:7–12 and Mark's Christology," *JBL* 84 (1965):
341–51.

Only the reference to Jesus' ascending mountains and his withdrawing to his house or any house supports the idea that the Markan Jesus intentionally chooses seclusion to address special teachings to his disciples. The pattern that emerges from the house motif is at best confused. While it is true that on occasion a house is the locus for Jesus' private instruction to his disciples (7:17; 9:28, 33; 10:10), it is more often than not a location for the revelation of Jesus' ministry to "outsiders" (2:1 ff., 15; 3:20–35; 7:24 ff.; 14:3 ff.).

It cannot be denied that many of the references to a house as a place of secrecy can be attributed to Mark's redaction (7:17, 24; 8:26; 9:33; 10:10). This fact, along with the obvious Markan statement in 9:30 about Jesus' desire to remain incognito argues impressively for the fact that a secrecy motif is functioning behind certain references to Jesus' cloistering of himself in houses (a la Wrede). I believe it can be explained in terms of Mark's polemic against the esoteric gospel of his enemies. In advocating a secret gospel the enemies in all likelihood claimed, regardless of Mark's protestations, that Mark and his suffering-servant christology are wrong, that Mark does not have the authentic gospel because he has never been exposed to the secret gospel of Jesus. According to this line of argument, Jesus imparted the true gospel to his disciples in secret (4:11–12), a gospel now in the possession of Mark's enemies. Mark, the opponents would then claim, has imparted christological half-truths because he has never been instructed in the whole truth, the secret instruction which they, the "successors" to the disciples, possess. Thus, in their contention, Mark's arguments against them are disqualified, for he does not have all the kerygmatic facts.

To counteract this Mark had to show that there was nothing more in the teaching of Jesus to his disciples than what became manifest to those on the outside. To prove this he plays his enemies' game by narrating the fact that

Jesus did instruct his disciples privately in teachings that were not heard by outsiders. But instead of the content of this secret teaching being the gospel (ὁ λόγος) the enemies claim it is, it turns out that the gospel Jesus imparts in private in a house to the disciples (7:17 ff.; 9:30–37; 10:10 ff., 32–45) is the same gospel which he proclaims and manifests in public (7:14 ff.; 8:34–35; 10:13 ff., 17 ff.; 12:41 ff.; 15:20–41), namely, the gospel of suffering christology and discipleship.

With respect to Jesus' use of a mountain for revelation the same explanation holds true. Again, like the house, a mountain becomes the locus of Jesus' secret instruction to his disciples (3:13 ff.; 9:2 ff.; 13:3 ff.); but again it is not because Mark is interested in picturing Jesus as one who gives instruction to his disciples in private which cannot be known to the "outsiders" (cf. 8:34–9:1 and 13:9–32). Mark narrates "the private mountain instruction" of Jesus only to discredit the argument of his *theios-aner* opponents. Contrary to their claims, the Markan Jesus does not teach anything in private that he does not reveal in public. The content of Jesus' public and private instruction is Jesus' suffering christology and the call of his disciples to take up the cross of suffering discipleship.

Conclusion

From the results of this study of Mark the following reconstruction of the Markan *Sitz im Leben* emerges. The writer's community finds itself at the beginning of the eighth decade A.D. faced with a crisis of faith. Forty years have passed since Easter morning. The expectations and hopes generated in the Christian community as a result of that event have not been realized. Easter has come and gone the old world order still continues. The eschatological age has dawned, but inexplicably the eschatological day of final consummation and reckoning has not irrupted. Jesus has not returned to his community of believers as the triumphant and gloried Son of man. The joys of the kingdom of God are still only dreamed of. In the course of this interim period the Markan church has been beset by suffering and persecution.

Mark, troubled by this state of affairs, has sought solace and strength to persevere in two ways. First, like Paul, he has turned to a christology that makes sense of the price of discipleship in his day. In a church faced with suffering he has adopted a positive attitude toward suffering and affirmed it as the authentic course of messiahship and discipleship. The focus of this spiritual reflection is on the suffering life-style of Jesus. The cross for Mark has become the crucial christological event for understanding Jesus as well as Christian existence. Mark also has found strength to persevere in this cross path of Christian existence in his convictions that Jesus will return momentarily, exalted and triumphant. Our evangelist is convinced that the returning Lord will vindicate the belief in him as the suffering servant and in the legitimacy of cross discipleship.

Recently Mark's position has been put to the most severe test it has faced. A new christological position has swept through the community. Certain interlopers have arrived proclaiming a *theios-aner* christology. The threat that this *theios-aner* position brings to Mark and his kerygma is absolutely devastating.

On almost every count the *theioi andres* present a different understanding of Jesus and Christian existence than what Mark himself has preached. The interlopers talk about Jesus as a great miracle worker, as one who imparted secret teachings about God and himself, as one who can be experienced as the exalted Lord, if the believer cultivates his spiritual life to the high pitch of spiritual ecstasy. They argue that authentic faith is evidenced in a person by a demonstration of great miracle-working ability and by his ability to have pneumatic experiences of the exalted Lord. To back up their claims they have brought with them impressive data. They have brought stories of Jesus: of his miracle working, of his disputes with his enemies,[1] of his death, which for them was not an event of desolation or despair but a triumphant event in which Jesus became exalted and victorious over the blind rulers of the world who crucified him. Fashioning their hermeneutic with the aid of Isaiah 6:9–10, these interlopers argue that not every-

---

1. I concur with Johannes Schreiber, *Theologie des Vertrauens* (Hamburg: Furche-Verlag H. Rennebach K. G., 1967), pp. 73 ff., that the interest in narrating and collecting epiphany stories began in a Christian circle which sought to establish Jesus as a *theios aner* for missionary and cultic interests in the Hellenistic world. It is, as Schreiber contends, not unlikely that the Stephen circle may have initiated this new departure in the Christian kerygma. Leander Keck, "Mark 3:7–12 and Mark's Christology," *JBL* 84 (1965): 341–59, has convincingly identified two different cycles of miracle stories in the first half of Mark. One operates under the rubric of "the strong man"; the other clearly establishes Jesus as a *theios aner* and consists of two clusters of stories, one with a boat motif, and the other with a touch motif. Both cycles, I believe, belonged to Mark's opponents. A great deal of work needs to be done to isolate all the material which belonged to Mark's opponents. However, the task is beyond the scope of this investigation.

one can understand the mystery of God, the secret gospel—
which they possess. In fact, the world proves itself blind
to the meaning of Jesus. To the world Jesus' life and
death remains forever a riddle (παραβολή). But to those
introduced to the secret gospel (ὁ λόγος), Jesus' life and
death are the message of salvation. The truth of this gospel
is guaranteed, so these *theioi andres* claim, because it is the
same gospel which Jesus delivered to the disciples and
which the disciples, in turn, delivered to them.[2]

These recent interlopers into Mark's community are surprised to find that his community is so distressed over the
absence of the exalted Lord. They know only of the ecstasy
of union with the exalted Lord in their own experience.
They are surprised, too, to find the community struggling
so with the problem of suffering and persecution, to the
point that it has been driven to find some positive value in
suffering as the mark of authentic Christian existence. They
recognize that suffering and persecution are present realities
in this world, but they see no reason to become obsessed
with them, as Mark's community has. They see instead
what for them is a much more powerful and joyful dimension to the faith. They find strength in their constant
union with their exalted Lord. Moreover, they have discovered the power and success of miracle working. This
for them is the powerful proof of the faith, the aspect of
the Christian movement that dazzles unbelievers and brings
converts into the fold, as well as honor and esteem to themselves. Consonant with the discovery of the benefits of viewing the faith from a *theios-aner* perspective, they have developed a *theios-aner* christology. In their theology Jesus
is a great *theios aner* in a long line of *theioi andres*. Christologically, Jesus is the *theios aner* God chose to be his Christ,
a fact unquestionably demonstrated, so Mark's opponents
claim, in Peter's resurrection experience (9:2–8).

---

2. In this aspect these *theioi andres* are similar to their *theios-aner* cousins
who circulated the Signs Source. They, too, claimed that the authenticity
of their kerygma was rooted in the tradition of the disciples (John 20:30).

This new perspective on Christian life is received with great enthusiasm by Mark's church. For those struggling with the insufferable character of Christian tribulation, unable to explain why Jesus has not returned and ended the abominable conditions of this world and inaugurated God's kingdom, the *theios-aner* position offers a new lease on Christian life.

For Mark the *theios-aner* perspective offers not life but spiritual death. He sees the *theios-aner* kerygma as a heresy, which will vitiate and undermine the faith. Its threat to Christian life is far greater than the external attacks on the Christian movement. For the sake of his community and the gospel itself, Mark decides that these heretics who have infiltrated his community have to be silenced and their position unmistakably discredited.

But at this point Mark is faced with a dilemma. How is he to silence his enemies and expose their position as heresy? His opponents have claimed an unimpeachable authority for their position: their kerygma was passed on to them by the disciples themselves. How can Mark over-trump that kind of claim to authenticity? Had he been Paul, he might have addressed his community much the same as Paul did, staking his own apostolic credentials against the impressive credentials of his opponents. But Mark is not Paul. Mark cannot claim such authority. If he addresses himself to the crisis by staking his own position as a Christian over against that of the disciples, he will be laughed down. Mark has to find someone with status and authority greater than the disciples' to argue his case and make it credible in the eyes of his community.

There is only one authority with status greater than that of the disciples to which Mark can appeal: the historical Jesus! He alone can expose the heresy of Mark's *theios-aner* opponents and make that exposition believable, while at the same time confirming the authenticity of Mark's kerygma. It is to Jesus that Mark turns.

In a stroke of genius Mark decides to dramatize the christological dispute raging between himself and his opponents through the interrelation of Jesus with his disciples during the course of the public ministry. That is, he stages the christological debate of his community in a "historical" drama in which Jesus serves as a surrogate for Mark and the disciples serve as surrogates for Mark's opponents. Jesus preaches and acts out the Markan suffering-servant theology. The disciples promulgate and act out *theios-aner* theology.

With consummate skill, Mark demonstrates to the reader that the disciples, far from being sympathetic to and understanding Jesus' messiahship, are obtuse, obdurate, and obstinate men who finally reject Jesus as completely as the Jewish hierarchy. The evangelist produces this result by creating three successive stages in the disciples' relationship to Jesus. In the first stage they are unperceptive of practically all the unusual qualities and capabilities Jesus possesses (1:16—8:26).[3] Others flock to Jesus because they perceive that Jesus possesses great miraculous powers. The disciples are oblivious and unresponsive even to this dimension of Jesus.

The second stage is marked by a period of misconception (8:27—14:9). At this point in the drama the insight that Jesus has messianic potential dawns on the disciples. Jesus admits to a claim to messiahship but not to the kind of Messiah the disciples envision. They want Jesus to be a *theios-aner* Messiah. Jesus refuses to choose any other messianic path but suffering servanthood. The impasse produces conflict between the disciples and Jesus from that point on over matters concerning both christology and discipleship.

Finally, the third stage in the disciples' relationship with Jesus is introduced with Judas' plan for betrayal and is marked by the disciples' total and unqualified rejection of Jesus (14:10–72).[4]

3. Leander Keck, "The Introduction to Mark's Gospel," *NTS* 12 (1966): 352–70, has successfully argued that Mark's introduction extends through 1:15. It is with 1:16 that Mark begins the main body of his work, that is, with the introduction of the disciples.
4. Once he has shown their apostasy, 1:16–14:72, he concludes his narrative with Pilate's judgment against Jesus and Jesus' crucifixion, burial, and resurrection.

As the reader becomes engrossed in the evangelist's schematization, the "history" of the disciples' relationship with Jesus makes Mark's point crystal clear. The disciples are reprobates. They obstinately hold on to a christology that Jesus has branded as heretical. In rejecting Jesus they themselves are rejected (8:38). They are no more than heretics. In Mark's schema the disciples remain heretics even unto his own day.

After Jesus' resurrection the possibility that they might be forgiven and restored to their place in the Christian community, according to Mark, never materialized. They never received the resurrection message (16:6–8). They were never rehabilitated. Mark's obvious message to his own community is this: those who persist in the *theios-aner* position of messiahship and discipleship persist in a view that Jesus himself rejected before his crucifixion. It is the view of the blind, obdurate disciples that leads to self-excommunication from the true faith. It is a theological cancer that must be destroyed, lest it vitiate and weaken authentic commitment to Christian existence.

The success of Mark's polemic against his enemies lies in part in the way he was able to turn his opponents' own tradition against them. He collects their epiphany stories in which Jesus is dramatized as a miracle worker and narrates them in the first half of his Gospel, prior to the Petrine confession. One would think that by this impressive amassing of evidence of Jesus' miracle-working ability, the author wishes the reader to identify Jesus as a *theios-aner* Christ. Not at all. The *theios-aner* position is set up only to be discredited by Jesus once the disciples confess to that position.[5]

5. Mark saturates the first half of his Gospel with *theios-aner* miracle activity of Jesus. Once the evangelist has set up the *theios-aner* Christ position to destroy it, he no longer emphasizes *theios-aner* traits of Jesus in his narrative. Ulrich Luz, "Das Geheimnismotiv die Markanische Christologie," ZNW 56 (1965): 25, in pointing out that the wonder history predominates in the first half of the Gospel but is absent in the second half, contends that the two exceptions to this schema (9:14–29; 10:46–52) should not even be viewed as miracle stories but as illustrations of the

Mark takes the hermeneutical principle of his enemies (4:11–12), which sets them apart from others as select and secretly enlightened Christians, and turns this hermeneutical principle against them in a polemic which points up not the enlightenment of the *theios-aner* position but its blindness. He takes his opponents' term for gospel, empties it of its secretive and allegorical thrust, and uses it both to affirm his own Gospel and to polemicize against his opponents' use of the term and its content. He takes his opponents' christological title, *Son of God*, empties it of its *theios-aner* connotation, and associates it with the suffering Son-of-man christology, thereby turning it into a title appropriate for his own theology. He takes his opponents' Petrine resurrection story, which serves as the basis for their *theios-aner* resurrection faith, and turns it into a public-ministry story which attacks the *theios-aner* position and affirms Mark's Son-of-man christology.

Perhaps the most exemplary and skillful way in which Mark eviscerates his enemies' position by using their own material can be seen in the composition of the crucifixion narrative. Earlier we saw that Schreiber had been able to divide the crucifixion story into two traditions.[6] One tradition, a primitive Palestinian tradition consisting of 15:20b–22, 24, 27, spoke of Jesus' death in the terms of the death of a suffering righteous one. The other tradition, consisting of 15:25, 26, 29a, 32c, 33, 34a, 37, 38, portrayed Jesus' death not as a humiliating experience but as the triumph of a *theios aner* over his enemies. Mark takes this latter tradition, which belongs to his enemies, and by blending it with the primitive Palestinian tradition and his own redactional

---

disciples' relation to Jesus and of the nature of discipleship. It is not correct, however, to suggest that Mark has removed all *theios-aner* traits of Jesus in the last half of the Gospel. Certainly these traits are present in the transfiguration (9:2–8), in 9:14–29; 10:46–52, in the Palm Sunday experience, and in certain aspects of the passion narrative. But it is certainly accurate to say that these traits have been reduced to a low key, if not neutralized entirely, by the strong emphasis upon Jesus' messianic commitment to suffering servanthood.

6. See above, pp. 145–46.

creations (15:23, 29b, 30–32b, 34b–36, 39–41) completely changes the position on the crucifixion reflected in his enemies' tradition to the story of the death of a suffering, humiliated Son of man, a la the passion predictions.[7]

A few observations on the way in which he accomplishes this literary feat underscore the effectiveness of Mark's attack upon his enemies' tradition. First, he adds Psalms 22:1 to his enemies' material at 15:34a, thereby changing what Schreiber claims was originally a *theios aner*'s cry of power, triumph, and judgment into a cry of a humiliated man despairing over God's abandoning him in his hour of suffering. Second, by affixing 15:35–36 after 15:34 Mark brilliantly dramatizes the contrasting attitudes toward life-style reflected in Jesus and the *theios-aner* perspective. In 15:35 the *theios-aner* mind-set misinterprets Jesus' cry of despair (15:34) as a call to Elijah, the *theios aner*, for help. The bystanders construe this cry of Jesus to be an indication that he is capitulating to their position, and they prepare themselves for a miracle.

Few times in the Gospel has Mark more incisively characterized the *theios-aner* christology and at the same time discredited it than in his insertion of 15:30–32b in his opponents' crucifixion material. In the penning of these verses the *theios-aner* position customarily advocated by Jesus' disciples is taken up in their absence by the enemies of Jesus at the foot of the cross. These enemies taunt Jesus with their "power" christology, claiming that if he will just come down from the cross they will believe he is who he says he is. All they want to see is a miracle

---

7. Schreiber, *Theologie*, pp. 41–49, has erroneously identified Mark's interests with the second crucifixion tradition. He argues that Mark casts his lot with the message of the *theios-aner* crucifixion narrative. All one has to do is reflect upon the Markan allusion to Isaiah 53 in such a passage as 10:45 (cf. 14:24) and to Mark's championing of the suffering-servant motif over the *theios-aner* motif in such passages as 8:31–38; 9:31–37; 10:34–45 to recognize almost instinctively that Mark's position is more akin to the theology of the primitive Palestinian crucifixion narrative than the second. The Markan additions in 15:20b–41 verify this judgment and illustrate, contra Schreiber, Mark's basic opposition to the *theios-aner*/exaltation theology of the *theios-aner* crucifixion story.

and they will be persuaded. A more crass representation of the *theios-aner* christology would be difficult to find. This christology pouring forth from the lips of those who crucified Jesus ought to be sufficient evidence in itself to discredit it. But Mark is not finished with his attack on the position.

In the wake of this *"theios-aner"* taunting of Jesus and the advocacy of *theios-aner* christology by Jesus' (and Mark's) opponents, Mark finally and completely eviscerates the intent of the opponents' crucifixion narrative and strikes a death blow to their christological claims by penning the confession of the centurion (15:39). Solely on the basis of Jesus' suffering and death the centurion confesses to Jesus' divine sonship. In contrast to the opponents of Jesus, who refuse to believe him until he demonstrates that he is a *theios-aner* Messiah (15:32), the centurion, ironically the symbol of might and power, believes Jesus to be the Son of God because he died as a suffering servant.[8]

Finally, through chapter 13 Mark has Jesus instruct the reader in Mark's community that any claim that he will return before the collapse of the cosmos is heresy. All those who claim such are false prophets who know only a false Christ. The Christian community, so the Markan Jesus declares, must recognize that it lives in a negative but necessary interim period (13:10) in which its faith will be severely tested. Those who persevere, who preach the authentic gospel (namely, the gospel which the Markan Jesus lives out before the reader's eyes) will be saved

8. Schreiber to the contrary, the centurion is not driven to the confession because he has experienced the exaltation. Schreiber argues this on the grounds that the cry of Jesus is a cry of exaltation. He insists that this is demonstrated by the fact that the centurion *sees* the cry of Jesus. That bit of logic is hard to follow. How can one *see* a cry? If the key to the centurion's experience had been the cry of Jesus, if this were the focal point of the centurion's attention, then Mark would have stated that the centurion *heard* and believed. The point of 15:39a is to inform the reader that the centurion in charge of Jesus' execution had observed the whole drama of suffering and humiliation surrounding Jesus' death (the mocking and derision of his enemies, his cry of despair, and so on). When he saw that Jesus *died* in this manner (as a suffering servant) he was moved by this tragic experience to claim paradoxically that he was the Son of God.

(13:10–13). They need not fear about their witness of faith in this period, for the spirit which animated Jesus and guided him into being the Messiah will come to them and guide them in authentic discipleship. When, according to the Markan Jesus, history has run its course, the cosmos collapses, and the spirit-world forces are destroyed, then God will exalt him in power and glory and the angels will be sent out to gather the elect for their reunion with Jesus (13:24–27).

It is in this way that Mark polemicizes against his opponents' position and reassures his community in their own faith. How successful Mark was we do not know. At best it was probably a limited victory. For even Mark must have had to make some concessions in his thinking to the *theios-aner* position. This was inevitable because of the very nature of his polemic. As soon as he introduced his opponents' material into his composition, his own position was compromised.[9] It was the price he had to pay to unmask his opponents' position and save the faith of his community. It was the same price Paul often had to pay to discredit his opponents' position and substantiate his own. It was the price Paul paid in Corinth in his polemics against the Gnostics of 1 Corinthians and the *theioi andres* of 2 Corinthians 2:14–7:4; 10–13. In each of these instances Paul drew upon the offensive theology of his opponents in order to use it in his polemic against them (e.g., 1 Corinthians 1:18–2:16; 2 Corinthians 3:7–18; 11:16–12:13). Once Paul used the terminology and argument of his opponents in his rebuttal of their position that terminology and theology colored his own theology in a way it had not been colored before. The same was true for Mark.

9. Likewise, the incorporation of their material in the service of his polemic against his opponents at points produces contradictions, or at best impressions at cross-purposes with his schematic intent. For example, while he wishes to convince the reader that the disciples are unperceptive to Jesus as a *theios aner* prior to the Petrine confession, his use of his opponents' material at 3:13–19; 6:7–13, 30 would suggest that the disciples must have viewed Jesus as a *theios aner*. For they accept the commission from him to be *theioi andres* and are successful.

Bibliography

Achtemeier, Paul J. "Toward the Isolation of Pre-Markan Miracle Catenae." *JBL* 89 (1970): 265–91.

Aune, David E. "The Problem of the Messianic Secret." *Nov Test* 11 (1969): 1–31.

Baird, J. Arthur. *Audience Criticism and the Historical Jesus*. Philadelphia: Westminster Press, 1969.

Baltensweiler, H. *Die Verklärung Jesu*. Zurich: Zwingli, 1959.

Beasley-Murray, G. R. *Jesus and the Future*. London: Macmillan & Co., 1954.

Betz, H. Dieter. "Jesus as Divine Man." *Jesus and the Historian*. Edited by F. Thomas Trotter. Colwell festschrift. Philadelphia: Westminster Press, 1965.

Bickerman, Elias. "Das leere Grab." *ZNW* 23 (1924): 281–92.

Bietenhard, Hans. "ὄνομα." *TDNT* 5: 242–83.

Boobyer, G. H. *St. Mark and the Transfiguration Story*. Edinburgh: T. & T. Clark, 1942.

Bornkamm, Günther. "μυστήριον." *TDNT* 4: 802–27.

———; Barth, Gerhard; and Held, H. J. *Tradition and Interpretation in Matthew*. Translated by Percy Scott. Philadelphia: Westminster Press, 1963.

Brun, Lyder. *Die Auferstehung Christi in der urchristlichen Ueberlieferung*. Oslo: H. Aschehoug & Co. (W. Nygaard), 1925.

Bultmann, Rudolf. *History of the Synoptic Tradition*. Translated by John Marsh. Oxford: Basil Blackwell, 1963.

———. *Das Evangelium des Johannes*. 16th ed. Göttingen: Vandenhoeck and Ruprecht, 1959.

Burch, Ernest W. "Tragic Action in the Second Gospel: A Study in the Narrative of Mark." *JR* 11 (1931): 346–58.

Burkill, T. A. *Mysterious Revelation*. Ithaca, N. Y.: Cornell University Press, 1963.

169

Busch, Friedrich. *Zum Verständnis der synoptischen Eschatologie, Markus 13 neu untersucht.* Gütersloh: Bertelsmann, 1938.

Carlston, C. E. "Transfiguration and Resurrection." *JBL* 80 (1961) 233–40.

Conzelmann, Hans. "Geschichte und Eschaton nach Mk 13." *ZNW* 50 (1959): 210–21.

————. "Present and Future in the Synoptic Tradition." Translated by Jack Wilson. *JTC* 5 (1968): 26–44.

————. *The Theology of St. Luke.* Translated by Geoffrey Buswell. New York: Harper & Row, 1961.

Cranfield, C. E. B. *The Gospel According to Saint Mark.* Cambridge: Cambridge University Press, 1953.

Cullmann, Oscar. *Peter.* Translated by F. V. Filson. Philadelphia: Westminster Press, 1953.

Dibelius, Martin. *From Tradition to Gospel.* Translated by B. L. Woolf. New York: Charles Scribner's Sons, 1935.

Dinkler, Erich. "Petrusbekenntnis und Satanswort (Das Problem der Messianität Jesu)." *Zeit und Geschichte.* Edited by Erich Dinkler. Bultmann festschrift. Tübingen: J. C. B. Mohr, 1964.

Ebeling, H. J. *Das Messiasgeheimnis und die Botschaft des Marcus-Evangelisten.* Berlin: Alfred Töpelmann, 1939.

Evans, C. F. "I Will Go before You into Galilee." *JTS,* n.s. 5 (1954): 3–18.

Fascher, E. ΠΡΟΦΗΤΗΣ. Giessen: Alfred Töpelmann, 1927.

Finegan, J. *Die Überlieferung der Leidens—und Auferstehungsgeschichte Jesu.* Giessen: Alfred Töpelmann, 1934.

Fortna, Robert. *The Gospel of Signs.* Cambridge: Cambridge University Press, 1970.

Friedrich, G. "προφήτης." *TDNT* 6: 828–61.

Fuller, Reginald H. *The Foundations of New Testament Christology.* New York: Charles Scribner's Sons, 1965.

Georgi, Dieter. *Die Gegner des Paulus im 2. Korintherbrief.* Neukirchen-Vluyn: Neukirchener Verlag, 1964.

Glasson, T. Francis. *The Second Advent.* 2d ed. London: Epworth Press, 1947.

Gnilka, J. *Die Verstockung Israels.* Munich: Kösel, 1961.

Grass, Hans. *Ostergeschehen und Osterberichte*. 3d ed. Göttingen: Vandenhoeck and Ruprecht, 1964.

Grässer, Erich. "Jesus in Nazareth (Mark VI. 1–6a)." *NTS* 16 (1969): 1–23.

————. *Das Problem der Parusieverzögerung in den synoptischen Evangelien und der Apostelgeschichte*. Berlin: Alfred Töpelmann, 1957.

Grundmann, W. *Das Evangelium nach Markus*. Berlin: Evangelische Verlagsanstalt, 1959.

Hadas, M. L., and Smith, Morton. *Heroes and Gods*. New York: Harper & Row, 1965.

Haenchen, Ernst. *Die Apostelgeschichte*. 13th ed. Göttingen: Vandenhoeck and Ruprecht, 1961.

————. "Die Komposition von Mk VII 27–IX I und Par." *Nov Test* 6 (1963): 81–109.

————. *Der Weg Jesu*. 2d ed. Berlin: Walter de Gruyter & Co., 1968.

Hahn, Ferdinand. *Titles of Jesus in Christology*. Translated by Harold Knight and George Ogg. London: Lutterworth Press, 1969.

Hamilton, Neill Q. *Jesus for a No-God World*. Philadelphia: Westminster Press, 1969.

————. "Resurrection Tradition and the Composition of Mark." *JBL* 84 (1965): 415–21.

————. "Revolution and *Mark's* Alternative." Paper presented to the Society of Biblical Literature, New York, 1970.

Hartmann, Lars. *Prophecy Interpreted*. Translated by Neil Tomkinson. Coniectanea Biblica, New Testament Series I. Lund, Sweden: C. W. K. Gleerup, 1966.

Hennecke, Edgar. *New Testament Apocrypha*. Vol. 2: *Writings Relating to the Apostles; Apocalypses and Related Subjects*. Edited by Wilhelm Schneemelcher. English translation edited by R. McL. Wilson. 2 vols. Philadelphia: Westminster Press, 1965.

Jeremias, Joachim. "Ἡλ(ε)ίας." *TDNT* 2: 928–41.

————. *The Eucharistic Words of Jesus*. Translated by Norman Perrin. New York: Charles Scribner's Sons, 1966.

————. *Jerusalem in the Time of Jesus*. Translated by F. H. Cave and C. H. Cave. Philadelphia: Fortress Press, 1969.

————. "Μωυσῆς." *TDNT* 4: 848–73.

————. *The Parables of Jesus.* Translated by S. H. Hooke. Rev. ed. New York: Charles Scribner's Sons, 1963.

Kähler, Martin. *The So-called Historical Jesus and the Historic, Biblical Christ.* Edited and translated by C. E. Braaten. Philadelphia: Fortress Press, 1964.

Käsemann, Ernst. *New Testament Questions of Today.* Translated by W. J. Montague. Philadelphia: Fortress Press, 1969.

Keck, Leander. "Mark 3:7–12 and Mark's Christology." *JBL* 84 (1965): 341–58.

————. "The Introduction to Mark's Gospel." *NTS* 12 (1966):352–70.

Klein, Günter. "Die Verleugnung des Petrus." *ZTK* 5 (1961), 285–328.

Klostermann, Erich. *Das Markusevangelium.* Handbuch zum Neuen Testament. 4th ed. Tübingen: J. C. B. Mohr (Paul Siebeck), 1950.

Klostermann, Erich. *Das Markusevangelium.* Handbuch zum Neuen 13–23.

Koester, Helmut. "Häretiker im Urchristentum." *RGG³* 3 (1959): 17–21.

————. "One Jesus and Four Primitive Gospels." *HTR* 61 (1968): 203–47.

————. "The Purpose of the Polemic of a Pauline Fragment." *NTS* 8 (1962): 317–32.

Kuby, Alfred. "Zur Konzeption des Markus-Evangeliums." *ZNW* 49 (1958): 52–64.

Kümmel, W. G. *Promise and Fulfillment.* Translated by Dorothea M. Barton. London: S. C. M. Press, 1957.

Lambrecht, Jan. *Die Redaktion der Markus-Apokalypse.* Analecta Biblica, no. 28. Rome: Pontifical Biblical Institute, 1967.

Lightfoot, R. H. *Locality and Doctrine in the Gospels.* London: Hodder & Stoughton, 1938.

————. *The Gospel Message of Mark.* Oxford: Clarendon Press, 1950.

Lindars, Barnabas. *New Testament Apologetic.* Philadelphia: Westminster Press, 1961.

Linnemann, E. *Jesus of the Parables.* Translated by J. Sturdy. New York: Harper & Row, 1966.

Livius, Titus. *Ab Urbe Condita. Livy.* Translated by B. O. Foster. Loeb Classical Library. London: William Heinemann, 1919.

Lohmeyer, Ernest. *Das Evangelium des Markus.* 15th ed. Göttingen: Vandenhoeck and Ruprecht, 1959.

————. *Galiläa und Jerusalem.* Göttingen: Vandenhoeck and Ruprecht, 1936.

————. "Die Verklärung Jesu nach dem Markus-Evangelium." *ZNW* 21 (1922): 185–215.

Luz, Ulrich. "Das Geheimnismotiv und die Markanische Christologie." *ZNW* 56 (1965): 9–30.

Manson, T. W. *The Teaching of Jesus.* London: Cambridge University Press, 1945.

Marrou, H. I. *A History of Education in Antiquity.* Translated by George Lamb. New York: Sheed and Ward, 1956.

Martyn, J. Louis. *History and Theology in the Fourth Gospel.* New York: Harper & Row, 1969.

Marxsen, Willi. *Mark the Evangelist.* Translated by R. A. Harrisville et al. Nashville, Tenn.: Abingdon Press, 1969.

————. "Redaktionsgeschichtliche Erklärung der sogenannten Parabeltheorie des Markus." *ZTK* 52 (1955): 255–71.

Meye, Robert P. *Jesus and the Twelve.* Grand Rapids, Mich.: William B. Eerdmans Publishing Co., 1968.

Moore, A. L. *The Parousia in the New Testament.* Leiden: E. J. Brill, 1966.

Oepke, A. "Der Herrnspruch über die Kirche Matth. 16: 17–19 in der neuesten Forschung," *ST* 2 (1950): 110–165.

Perrin, Norman. "The Christology of Mark: A Study in Methodology." A paper presented at the Seminar on Christology of the New Testament at th Annual Meeting of the Studiorum Novi Testamenti Societas, New Castle upon Tyne, England, August 1970.

————. "The Creative Use of the Son of Man Tradition by Mark." *USQR* 18 (1968): 357–65.

————. "Mark 14:62; End Product of a Christian Pesher Tradition?" *NTS* 12 (1965): 150–55.

————. *Rediscovering the Teaching of Jesus.* New York: Harper & Row, 1967.

————. "Towards an Interpretation of the Gospel of Mark." An unpublished paper.

————. *What Is Redaction Criticism?* Philadelphia: Fortress Press, 1969.

Pesch, Rudolf. *Naherwartungen.* Düsseldorf: Patmos, 1968.

Quesnell, Quentin. *The Mind of Mark.* Analecta Biblica, no. 38. Rome: Pontifical Biblical Institute, 1969.

Rawlinson, A. E. J. *St. Mark.* London: Methuen and Co., 1925.

Riddle, D. W. *The Gospels: Their Origin and Growth.* Chicago: University of Chicago Press, 1939.

Robinson, James M. "Basic Shifts in German Theology." *Int* 16 (1962): 76–97.

————. "Kerygma and History in the New Testament." *The Bible in Modern Scholarship.* Edited by J. P. Hyatt. Nashville, Tenn.: Abingdon Press, 1965.

————. "On the *Gattung* of Mark (and John)." *Jesus and Man's Hope.* Edited by D. G. Buttrick. A Perspective Book. Pittsburgh: Pittsburgh Theological Seminary, 1970.

————. *The Problem of History in Mark.* Naperville, Ill.: Allenson, 1957.

————. "The Problem of History in Mark, Reconsidered." *USQR* 20 (1965): 131–47.

————. "The Recent Debate on the 'New Quest.'" *JBR* 30 (1962): 198–218.

Robinson, J. A. T. *Jesus and His Coming.* Nashville, Tenn.: Abingdon Press, 1957.

Rohde, Joachim. *Rediscovering the Teaching of the Evangelists.* Translated by D. Barton. Philadelphia: Westminster Press, 1968.

Schenke, Ludger. *Auferstehungsverkündigung und leeres Grab.* Stuttgarter Bibelstudien, no. 33. Stuttgart: Katholisches Bibelwerk, 1969.

Schmidt, K. L. "Die Stellung der Evangelien in der allgemeinen Literaturgeschichte." ΕΥΧΑΡΙΣΤΗΡΙΟΝ. Edited by H. Schmidt. Vol. 2. Göttingen: Vandenhoeck and Ruprecht, 1923.

Schniewind, J. *Das Evangelium nach Markus.* Göttingen: Vandenhoeck and Ruprecht, 1949.

Schreiber, Johannes. "Die Christologie des Markusevangelium." *ZTK* 58 (1961): 154–83.

————. *Theologie des Vertrauens.* Hamburg: Furche-Verlag H. Rennebach K. G., 1967.

Schulz, Siegfried. "Markus und das Alte Testament." *ZTK* 58 (1961): 185–97.

Schweizer, Eduard. "Anmerkungen zur Theologie des Markus." *Neotestamentica et Patristica.* Edited by W. C. van Unnik. Leiden: E. J. Brill, 1962.

———. *EGO EIMI.* Göttingen: Vandenhoeck and Ruprecht, 1939.

———. *The Good News According to Mark.* Translated by D. H. Madvig. Richmond, Va.: John Knox Press, 1970.

———. *Lordship and Discipleship.* 1st English ed. Naperville, Ill.: Alec R. Allenson, 1960.

———. "Mark's Contribution to the Quest of the Historical Jesus." *NTS* 10 (1964): 421–32.

———. "πνεῦμα, πνευματικός." *TDNT* 6: 389–451.

———. "Die theologische Leistung des Markus." *EvTh* 24 (1964): 337–55.

———. "Zur Frage des Messiasgeheimnisses bei Markus." *ZNW* 56 (1965): 1–8.

Scroggs, Robin. "The Exaltation of the Spirit by Some Early Christians." *JBL* 84 (1965): 359–73.

———. "Mark: Theologian of the Incarnation." An unpublished paper presented to the Society of Biblical Literature, New York, 1970.

Sjöberg, Erik. *Der verborgene Menschensohn in den Evangelien.* Lund, Sweden: C. W. K. Gleerup, 1955.

Stauffer, E. "ἐγώ." *TDNT* 2: 343–62.

Strecker, Georg. "The Passion and Resurrection Predictions in Mark's Gospel." *Int* 22 (1968): 421–42.

———. *Der Weg der Gerechtigkeit.* Göttingen: Vandenhoeck and Ruprecht, 1966.

Suhl, Alfred. *Die Funktion der alttestamentlichen Zitate und Anspielungen im Markusevangelium.* Gütersloh: G. Mohn, 1965.

Talbert, Charles. *Luke and the Gnostics.* Nashville, Tenn.: Abingdon Press, 1966.

Taylor, Vincent. *The Gospel According to Mark.* London: Macmillan and Co., 1959.

Teeple, Howard. *The Mosaic Eschatological Prophet.* Philadelphia: Society of Biblical Literature, 1957.

Thrall, Margaret. "Elijah and Moses in Mark's Account of the Transfiguration." *NTS* 16 (1970): 305–17.

Tödt, H. E. *The Son of Man in the Synoptic Tradition.* Translated by D. M. Barton. Philadelphia: Westminster Press, 1965.

Trocmé, Étienne. *La Formation de l'Évangile selon Marc.* Paris: Presses Universitaires de France, 1963.

Tyson, Joseph. "The Blindness of the Disciples in Mark." *JBL* 80 (1961): 261–68.

Via, Dan, Jr. *The Parables: Their Literary and Existential Dimension.* Philadelphia: Fortress Press, 1967.

Vielhauer, Philipp. "Erwägungen zur Christologie des Markusevangeliums." *Zeit und Geschichte.* Edited by Erich Dinkler. Bultmann festschrift. Tübingen: J. C. B. Mohr, 1964.

Votaw, C. W. "The Gospels and Contemporary Biographies." *AJT* 19 (1915): 45–73, 217–49.

Walsh, P. G. *Livy: His Historical Aims and Methods.* London: Cambridge Press, 1961.

Weiss, Johannes. *Das älteste Evangelium.* Göttingen: Vandenhoeck and Ruprecht, 1903.

Wilckens, Ulrich. *Die Missionsreden Apostelgeschichte.* Neukirchen-Vluyn: Neukirchener Verlag, 1961.

Williams, C. S. C. *Alterations to the Text of the Synoptic Gospels and Acts.* Oxford: Alden Press, 1961.

Wrede, William. *Das Messiasgeheimnis in den Evangelien.* 3d ed. Göttingen: Vandenhoeck and Ruprecht, 1963.

Index of Authors

Index of Scripture References